MODERN
PASTA SAUCES

MODERN PASTA SAUCES

Delicious and Creative Twists on Your Favorite Classic Recipes

PAULA JONES

Photography by Elysa Weitala

ROCKRIDGE
PRESS

Interior and Cover Designer: Antonio Valverde
Art Producer: Michael Hardgrove
Editor: Emily Angell
Production Editor: Andrew Yackira
Photography © 2019 Elysa Weitala.
Food styling by Victoria Woollard.
Author photo courtesy of © Laura Oliver of Ransom Photography.
Cover: Roasted Beet Pesto

ISBN: Print 978-1-64152-990-7 | eBook 978-1-64152-991-4

R0

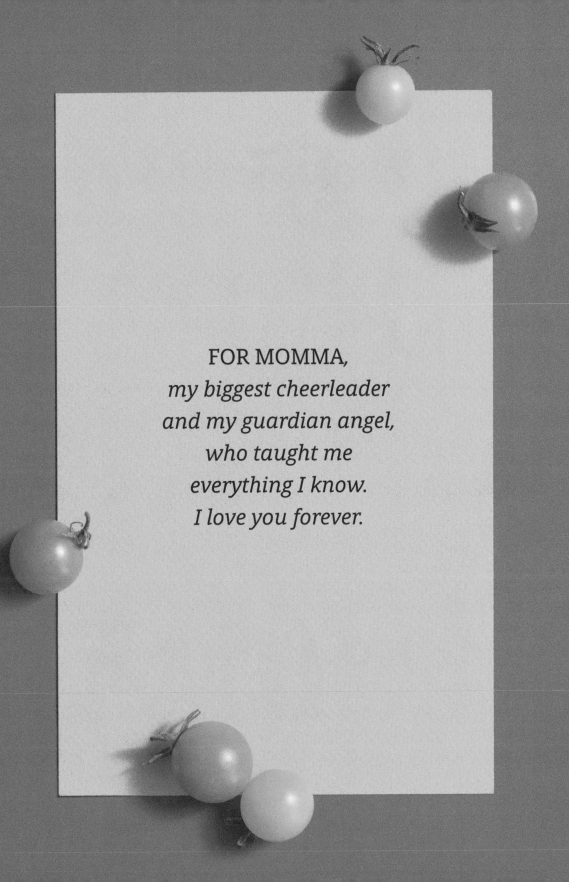

FOR MOMMA,
*my biggest cheerleader
and my guardian angel,
who taught me
everything I know.
I love you forever.*

CONTENTS

CHAPTER 6 MEAT · 69

CHAPTER 7 VEGAN · 83

INTRODUCTION

WELCOME! I'M SO GLAD YOU'RE HERE. I'm guessing if you have this book, you love Italian food as much as I do. I've been cooking for as long as I can remember—ever since I was tall enough to stand on a chair in the kitchen and stir. I love to cook all types of food, but I really have a passion for Italian food.

My father was a career military man, and he's where my love of travel comes from, as well as my love for Italian food. Our family was stationed in northern Italy, in the Friuli Venezia Giulia region, which is located at the top of the boot near the Alps, just above Venice. It's everything you would imagine it to be and more. I fell hard and fast for all things Italian. The culture, the people, the language, the architecture, and especially the food.

I dove into everything headfirst. Once I learned to speak Italian, I would pick up Italian cooking magazines and read them like textbooks, translating recipes for my

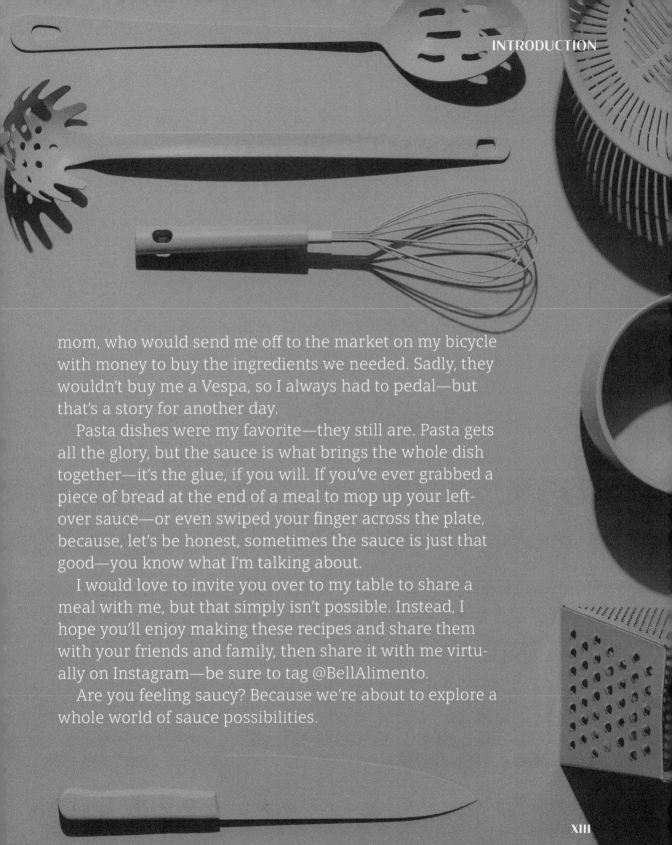

mom, who would send me off to the market on my bicycle with money to buy the ingredients we needed. Sadly, they wouldn't buy me a Vespa, so I always had to pedal—but that's a story for another day.

Pasta dishes were my favorite—they still are. Pasta gets all the glory, but the sauce is what brings the whole dish together—it's the glue, if you will. If you've ever grabbed a piece of bread at the end of a meal to mop up your left-over sauce—or even swiped your finger across the plate, because, let's be honest, sometimes the sauce is just that good—you know what I'm talking about.

I would love to invite you over to my table to share a meal with me, but that simply isn't possible. Instead, I hope you'll enjoy making these recipes and share them with your friends and family, then share it with me virtually on Instagram—be sure to tag @BellAlimento.

Are you feeling saucy? Because we're about to explore a whole world of sauce possibilities.

WHAT'S
A MODERN SAUCE?

As the name implies, this cookbook focuses on pasta sauces as the star of the dish. While the sauces in this book are based on familiar Italian sauce recipes, each contains a creative twist using fresh, inventive, and yet approachable and accessible ingredients, and can all be made relatively quickly. These are not your Nonna's recipes—think Lentil Bolognese and Squash Carbonara.

WHAT'S
INSIDE THIS BOOK?

Inside this book, you'll find 60 versatile pasta sauce recipes built on familiar sauce bases: tomato, cream, meat, oil, pesto—there's even a vegan chapter. The recipes focus on fresh, whole ingredients when possible. When fresh is not possible, I offer substitution options. When I think about these recipes as a whole, *approachable* is a word that comes to mind, meaning you won't be stuck in the kitchen for hours prepping and cooking or running around town looking for expensive, hard-to-find ingredients. Our lives are busy enough—we don't need to complicate them further.

If you like lists as much as I do, you're in luck. You'll find a list of standard recommended pantry items in chapter 1. There, you'll find staples to have on hand to make the most out of the recipes in this book. A well-stocked pantry and refrigerator can be real time-savers.

Also included in chapter 1 is a helpful list of tools that you'll use on a regular basis to make the recipes in this book. You'll also find a section on general tips to make yourself look like a rock star in the kitchen.

HOW TO
USE THIS BOOK

This book is a great go-to solution for fun weeknight dinners, with a few Sunday sauce recipes thrown in for good measure. A Sunday sauce recipe is simply a sauce that typically takes longer to pull together than a regular weeknight allows for, making it perfect for weekends and occasions when you have more time to cook.

There is a diverse selection of pasta sauce recipes that are sure to be crowd-pleasers. They're broken down into six chapters: Oil, Tomato, Cream, Pesto, Meat, and Vegan, followed by a Base Dishes chapter that will serve as inspiration for you to pair ten sauces with pasta, meats, and perhaps a side or two.

The Resources section toward the end of the book is where I've listed cookbooks and websites that I recommend you check out. An index is included as well, so you can easily find recipes and ingredients.

CHAPTER 1

BEFORE YOU START

I F YOU ASK ME, THERE ISN'T ANYTHING BETTER THAN a big bowl of well-dressed (and by well-dressed, I mean perfectly sauced) pasta. I'm smiling just thinking about it. The key to the perfect pasta dish is the balance between the pasta and the sauce, as well as which sauces and pasta you pair together. You wouldn't want a pasta dish that's swimming in the wrong sauce. You also wouldn't want to choose a pasta that couldn't handle a specific sauce. The balance is part of the magic. You'll know you've gotten it just right when you take the first bite.

Pasta sauce has played an important role in Italian cooking for hundreds of years—and for good reason. Pasta sauce is the glue that binds a dish together and makes it sing. Are you hearing *Volare, oh oh oh* in your head right now? Sauces are here to stay.

Many people immediately think of a tomato-based sauce as the quintessential Italian sauce, but there are as many sauces as there are regions.

Ragù alla Bolognese may be one of the most famous Italian pasta sauces. Bolognese is a meat-based sauce from Bologna, Italy. It is a slowly cooked sauce requiring different techniques and is simmered to a thick, rich texture. Bolognese can be served over many different forms of pasta or baked into lasagna.

The decadent carbonara sauce from Rome is made of eggs, cheese, pancetta or *guanciale*, and black pepper, and is a newer sauce created in the mid-20th century. It is believed this heavy sauce was created to keep coal miners—*carbonaro*—full for a long, hard day of labor. Predecessors of this sauce may be *spaghetti alla gricia* (made with bacon, cheese, and pepper) and *cacio e uova* (melted lard and eggs mixed with cheese).

A classic, simple tomato sauce is always a favorite. Although tomato sauce may sound a bit boring, there are many ways to spruce it up. When simmered long enough, it becomes a silky and satisfying topping for any al dente pasta.

Additionally, each region in Italy puts its own unique spin on classic sauces.

Southern Italians embrace tangy tomato sauces, while making the most of Italy's abundance of olive oils.

Northern Italian chefs stir up butter-based sauces rich with cream, garlic, and an array of fresh herbs.

As is the case in most countries, there are regional sauce specialties that can even vary from family to family. Naturally, every family claims their version is the best. Here's a secret: the best version is the one that *you* like the most.

With that said, certain pasta sauces are better suited to specific pasta. For instance, a chunky meat sauce like a Bolognese is best paired with thick hearty noodles like lasagna, pappardelle, and large shells or tubes. Delicate thin pasta (such as angel-hair/vermicelli or thin spaghetti) work well with light cream sauces. Filled pastas like ravioli and tortellini are big on flavor, so they work well with oil- or butter-based sauces. Short twisted pasta like fusilli or cavatappi pair beautifully with pesto that clings to the curves. Macaroni, rigatoni, and penne pasta scream out for baked dishes heavy on cheese sauces. While these are all examples of classic pairings, many of these pasta/sauce combos can be interchanged based on what you have on hand and can be adjusted for vegetarians with quick substitutions. That's the beauty of Italian cooking! 🍎

STANDARD PANTRY

I'm a strong believer that having a well-stocked pantry and refrigerator will make your kitchen life easier and save you time and money in the long run. You'll be better prepared to pull together delicious meals quickly and easily no matter the time if you have a collection of pantry staples on hand. Late-night pasta cravings? Check. Friends or family popping by unannounced? No problem. Your mother-in-law announces she's gone vegan? You'll still have dinner on the table in a jiffy.

Once your pantry is stocked, there may not ever be a reason to order delivery or hit a drive-through again. Save that money you would've spent on takeout for a vacation and learn some delicious new recipes to top it all off.

This list of ingredients is a great place to start and will specifically help you make the most of the recipes in this book. I'll leave it up to you whether you want to break out the label maker and make your pantry "Pinterest pretty" or not.

INGREDIENTS

Kosher salt

Black pepper

Red pepper flakes

Extra-virgin olive oil

Milk

Heavy whipping cream

Sour cream

Vinegars (balsamic, red wine)

Quality jarred or
    canned artichokes

Quality canned tomatoes
    (crushed, diced,
    tomato sauce)

Sun-dried tomatoes

Tomato paste

Cheeses (Parmesan,
    goat, ricotta)

Bread crumbs/panko

Quality jarred roasted red
    bell peppers

Pastas (a selection of both
    short and long)

All-purpose flour

Eggs

Unsalted butter

Lentils

White beans (cannellini)

Chickpeas

Nuts (pine, cashews,
    walnuts, hazelnuts)

Capers

Wines (white and red)

Canned anchovies (or
    anchovy paste)

Olives

THE BENEFIT OF
FRESH, HIGH-QUALITY INGREDIENTS

Whether you're shopping for cream or eggs, tomatoes or citrus, leafy greens or herbs, fresh is the way to go.

Italian food is traditionally based on seasonality. Italians cook with what's in season or with foods they've canned and preserved from previous seasons. This is something that I believe in and do as well. When you're using what's in season, you're typically getting the freshest ingredients possible.

Where do you find seasonal items? If you don't have your own garden, there are many wonderful local farmers' markets popping up these days. Farmers are a wealth of knowledge—don't hesitate to ask about something you see in their stands. Visiting a farmers' market near the end of the day may win you discounts on produce farmers don't want to lug home. See if they will give you a deal on bruised or ugly produce—you're just going to cut it up anyway!

Of course, you can always shop at your local supermarket. Chopping and divvying up produce on your own will save a pretty penny; the precut veggies can be quite expensive. Also, consider planning your weekly menu around sales your local store is running that week and buy in bulk if the prices are good. Be sure to freeze whatever seasonal produce you can so you will have a wide variety of food available year-round.

Remember, what you put into a recipe matters: Quality ingredients in, quality results out. Whenever possible you'll want to seek out fresh, high-quality ingredients to use no matter what you're cooking. Your body will thank you for it. Here is a list to get you started:

Fresh tomatoes (Roma, cherry)

Fennel

Squash (butternut,
    pumpkin, zucchini)

Red bell peppers

Fresh mushrooms (portobello)

Fresh garlic

Kale

Cauliflower

Baby spinach

Beets

Onions (white, spring/green)

Leeks

Carrots

Celery

Eggplant

Fresh herbs (basil, thyme, sage,
    parsley, mint—you can sub-
    stitute dried herbs in a pinch)

Lemons

TOOLS

~~~~~~

In order to do any job well, you need the proper tools. I've compiled a list of tools you'll need to cook the majority of the recipes in this book.

CHEF'S KNIFE — In my opinion, the chef's knife is one of the most important kitchen tools and one of the best investments you can make. When shopping for a knife, choose one that feels comfortable and secure in your hand. Take into account the knife's weight, shape, and size. One size or brand does not fit all. Visit a cutlery store to try them before you buy them. Remember, what works for your neighbor, your favorite online food personality, or best friend may not work for you. Keep an open mind.

CUTTING BOARD — You'll need a nice cutting board, as well as flexible cutting mats, for all that chopping, dicing, and slicing in the kitchen. I gravitate to heavy, stable wooden cutting boards. As a bonus, they can last forever if you take good care of them.

PASTA POT (STOCKPOT) — It's hard to make pasta without a pasta pot or stockpot. You need a pot large enough to hold 4 to 6 quarts of water.

SAUCEPAN — We're getting saucy in this book, so you'll definitely need a saucepan. I like a large, heavy-bottomed pan or a small Dutch or French oven for this task.

SKILLET / CAST IRON SKILLET — Great for searing, browning, or frying foods. A kitchen workhorse. Just don't drop it on your foot!

COLANDER — Or strainer, depending on where you're from. If your pasta pot does not include a strainer, you'll need a separate colander to strain all the pasta you'll be cooking. There are several collapsible options on the market, if space is an issue.

CHEESE GRATER — Cheese is best when purchased whole and then grated as needed. Choose a grater that works for hard cheeses like Parmesan, Grana, or pecorino.

WOODEN SPOONS — Other humble workhorses of the kitchen. It's nice to have a few different sizes on hand.

LADLE — Use to ladle sauce and serve food.

MINI FOOD PROCESSOR — Comes in handy for large chopping tasks. You can, of course, do this with your chef's knife instead.

BLENDER — Not just for smoothies. Blenders are great for making smooth sauces and pesto. You don't need anything fancy.

TONGS — Tongs are a great multipurpose tool, allowing you to easily turn meat and vegetables. Some people even prefer to use tongs to transfer pasta from boiling water into a saucepan in place of a colander.

OVEN MITTS — Or gloves, to protect those creative hands.

GENERAL TIPS

~~~~~~~~~~~~~~~~~~~~~~~~~~~~~~~~~~~

Now you know which staples to have on hand in your pantry and refrigerator and which tools will serve you well as you begin experimenting with the recipes in this book. But before you head into the kitchen to get cooking, I'm going to share my 10 best tried-and-tested tips and tricks to help set you up for cooking success.

1   Start with a clean work area (and an empty dishwasher). Cleanliness is important to food safety and for giving yourself a clean, blank canvas on which to prepare a delicious meal. Make your area sparkle.

2   Read through the entire recipe prior to starting. It's best to know what steps come next. You don't want any surprises halfway through cooking.

3   Prepare and organize your ingredients and tools, a process known as *mise en place*. Really, it's just a fancy French culinary term that means "putting in place." Prepping everything ahead of time will make cooking so much easier. You don't want to have to stop mid-dish to chop an onion or wait for the cream to come to room temperature. Maybe line up ingredients in the order you will use them.

4   Wash your hands as often as necessary. Keep them clean all the way through.

5   Season foods well while you cook and taste as you go. This includes pasta water. Salt your boiling

~~~~~~~~~~~~~~~~~~~~~~~~~~~~~~~~~~~~~

water so it tastes like the sea—1 tablespoon of salt for every pound of pasta. If you use kosher salt, which I prefer, make it a heaping tablespoon. You can experiment and add another ½ to full tablespoon of salt, according to your preferences.

6 Don't overcook pasta. Pasta should be al dente (meaning "to the tooth, a little bite"). When you bite into it, your teeth should feel some resistance, but the pasta should still be tender. The only time I want to eat something gummy is when I'm digging into a bag of gummy bears.

7 Pasta water is magical. Set aside a cup of pasta water prior to draining your pasta, just in case you need it to mix with your sauce.

8 Don't crowd your pan. Cook in batches if you have to. Let your food breathe while it cooks for even cooking, browning, and searing.

9 Let meat "rest" for 10 to 20 minutes before slicing into it, depending on the size of the cut. Meat needs time to redistribute all the juicy flavors inside. Be patient. It will pay off.

10 Clean your dishes and prep area as you go. You'll be glad you did. No one wants to clean an entire kitchen with a belly full of *pasta amatriciana*.

CHAPTER 2

OIL

O LIVE OIL, OFTEN LOVINGLY REFERRED TO as liquid gold or liquid sunshine because of its gorgeous color, is an incredibly important part of Italian cooking. So important that I use it on a daily basis, not only as an enhancement of the cooking process, but as a finishing element to dishes as well. Naturally, this makes olive oil one of my highly treasured pantry staples.

There are many different types of oils one can use. I happen to keep a few different bottles of olive oils in my pantry at all times. First and foremost, I have extra-virgin olive oil (EVOO) for its full-bodied flavor. In addition, I like to keep a small variety of specialty olive oils in my kitchen: basil-infused olive oil, mandarin-infused olive oil, chili-infused olive oil, even a chocolate-infused olive oil. Specialty oils are typically used to finish dishes during plating and can really make a dish sing. You can find specialty infused oils in some markets, online, or you can even make your own.

This chapter is oil-forward. These are recipes that feature olive oil as the base of the sauce, and they can include infused oils or oil being used as a final finishing element during plating.

I prefer extra-virgin olive oil when making sauces, not only for its taste, but also for its complementary flavor to other ingredients. It will be the focus of the recipes in this section.

Let's get down to the nitty-gritty of this beloved pantry staple. There are a few things you should know about olive oils. As with most ingredients, all olive oils are not created equally. Olive oil is produced from, you guessed it, olives. After harvest, the olives are pressed and their oil is separated from the fruit. (Yes, olives are a fruit.) Different varieties of olives grow throughout Italy, and the oils they produce are just as varied. Depending on the region the olive oil hails from, the flavor profiles can be tangy, fruity, full-bodied, or light. The colors can also vary from greens to yellows. If that isn't enough variation, there are also different grades of olive oils. It's enough to make your head swim (in a good way), so for now, just know that for the majority of the recipes in this book we'll be using extra-virgin olive oil.

How you store olive oil is equally important. Olive oil should be kept in a sealed vessel/container. Since I never want to be without, I prefer a glass bottle so I can see exactly how much oil I have left before it's time to replenish. Olive oil should be stored in a cool dark place like a kitchen cupboard. While I realize that it would be super convenient to keep your olive oil next to your stove where you use it most, heat and light can negatively affect the life-span of your olive oil, so you'll want to avoid that. Tuck it away behind a cupboard door.

If stored properly after opening, the shelf life of olive oil is around six months. The trick Mom taught you about smelling things in the kitchen is a good one. Smell your olive oil, too: It should smell fragrant. If it smells rancid, toss it.

We'll be highlighting olive oil in this chapter, as well as continuing its use throughout the book to make classic recipes with fresh twists, like Aglio e Olio (garlic and oil) with Kale (page 20), plus a few modern takes on sauces that you may not have thought of, like my Blender Curried Chickpea Sauce (page 24). 🍎

Caramelized Mushroom Sauce with Thyme

SERVES 4

PREP TIME: 10 MIN
COOK TIME: 30 MIN

FLAVOR NOTES:
RICH, SAVORY

ONE POT, NUT FREE, VEGETARIAN (OPTION), GLUTEN FREE

4 tablespoons unsalted
  butter, divided

2 tablespoons extra-virgin olive oil

¼ onion, minced

2 cloves garlic, minced

8 ounces sliced baby
  portobello mushrooms

¼ teaspoon kosher salt

⅛ teaspoon freshly ground
  black pepper

1 cup chicken stock

1 teaspoon balsamic vinegar

1 or 2 stems fresh thyme

Parmesan cheese, grated (optional)

This sauce is rich and savory. It pairs beautifully with thick noodles, such as tagliatelle or pappardelle. This decadent sauce is cooked up in 30 minutes, but after one taste, you'll swear it took all day to develop such deliciousness. It's easy enough for a weeknight meal, yet elegant enough for company. If you're a mushroom lover, this is a must make.

1 Heat 2 tablespoons of butter and 2 tablespoons of olive oil in a 3.5- or 5-quart Dutch oven (or heavy-bottomed sauce-pan) over medium heat. Add the onion and garlic and cook until softened, stirring as necessary. Be careful not to let the garlic burn.

2 Add the mushrooms and season with salt and pepper. Cook until the mushrooms have softened, released their water, and have begun to brown.

3 Add the chicken stock and balsamic vinegar and stir to combine. Taste the seasoning and add additional ¼ teaspoon of salt and pepper to taste, if needed.

4 Add the remaining 2 tablespoons of butter, reduce heat to low, and cook until the sauce thickens.

5 Remove the thyme leaves from the stems and scatter leaves into the sauce. Garnish with a sprinkling of Parmesan cheese, if desired.

Substitution Tip You could easily make this dish vegetarian by swapping out the chicken stock for vegetable stock.

Storage Instructions Transfer any leftovers to an airtight container and store in the refrigerator for up to 4 days.

Quick Olive Oil and Parmesan Sauce with Bacon

SERVES 4

PREP TIME: 5 MIN
COOK TIME: 15 MIN

FLAVOR NOTE:
SAVORY

NUT FREE, ONE POT, KID FRIENDLY, 5 INGREDIENTS OR LESS, VEGETARIAN (OPTION), GLUTEN FREE, 30 MIN OR LESS

2 pieces thick-cut bacon, diced

½ cup extra-virgin olive oil

2 cloves garlic, minced

½ cup grated Parmesan cheese

1 tablespoon coarsely chopped fresh parsley (optional)

This quick olive oil and Parmesan sauce with crispy bacon crumbles is just that—QUICK. Not a lot of time? No problem. Less than five ingredients and about 15 minutes are all you need before you're twirling your fork around this classic comfort food in a bowl. I like to think of this dish as the grown-up version of buttered noodles with your favorite powdered cheese. It's sure to become a new family favorite.

1 Place the bacon in a 3.5- or 5-quart Dutch oven or saucepan and cook until crispy, stirring often. Using a slotted spoon, transfer the cooked bacon to a plate lined with paper towels or napkins. Discard the grease and carefully wipe your pan clean.

2 Heat the olive oil in the saucepan over medium heat. Add garlic and cook until fragrant, being careful not to burn the garlic.

3 Add the crispy bacon and Parmesan and toss to coat.

4 Garnish with parsley, if desired.

Substitution Tip Substitute pancetta for bacon or omit altogether for a vegetarian version.

Storage Instructions Transfer any leftovers to an airtight container and store in the refrigerator for up to 4 days.

Lemon, Basil, and Capers Sauce

SERVES 4

PREP TIME: 10 MIN
COOK TIME: 30 MIN

FLAVOR NOTES:
RICH, TANGY

ONE POT, NUT FREE, VEGETARIAN

2 tablespoons extra-virgin olive oil

2 tablespoons unsalted butter

1 tablespoon all-purpose flour

2 cloves garlic, minced

¼ teaspoon kosher salt

⅛ teaspoon freshly ground
 black pepper

2 tablespoons capers, drained

½ cup dry white wine

2 tablespoons lemon juice

1 tablespoon lemon zest

Drizzle basil-infused olive oil

*Bright, briny, and buttery (try saying that ten times fast)
Lemon, Basil, and Capers Sauce pairs well with linguine.
The lemon adds just the right amount of tang for a delicious dish. It's great with pasta on its own, or amp it up
with the addition of your favorite protein (chicken or fish
are both great options). The sauce is finished with a drizzle
of basil-infused olive oil, which brings it all together.*

1 Heat the oil and butter in a saucepan over medium heat.
   Add flour and whisk to combine.

2 Add the garlic, season with salt and pepper, and stir
   to combine.

3 Add the capers, wine, lemon juice, and lemon zest. Stir well
   to combine. Allow the sauce to continue cooking until the
   mixture thickens slightly.

4 Finish with a light drizzle of basil-infused olive oil.

Ingredient Tip If the mixture becomes too thick, thin with 1 tablespoon of
pasta water at a time until it reaches your desired consistency.
Storage Instructions Transfer any leftovers to an airtight container and
store in the refrigerator for up to 4 days.

Fresh Bread Crumb Pasta Sauce with Parsley

SERVES 4

PREP TIME: 5 MIN
COOK TIME: 15 MIN

FLAVOR NOTE:
SAVORY

**KID FRIENDLY, ONE POT,
VEGETARIAN, NUT FREE,
5-INGREDIENT, 30 MIN OR LESS**

3 tablespoons extra-virgin olive oil

3 cloves garlic, minced

1 teaspoon red pepper flakes

1 cup panko bread crumbs

¼ cup parsley, minced

Pecorino, grated, for garnish

Dare to be different with this delightfully quick and easy dish. This bread crumb pasta sauce is a carb-lover's dream. Bread and pasta in one dish? You bet. Think of how yummy a bread crumb topping is on baked mac and cheese. Long noodles, like spaghetti or bucatini, are tossed in a coating of garlic-flavored olive oil and then dressed with bread crumbs, herbs, and grated cheese. This one is hard to resist!

1 Heat oil in a saucepan over medium heat. Add the garlic and red pepper flakes and cook until fragrant, being careful not to burn the garlic.

2 Add the bread crumbs and stir until coated. Continue stirring until the bread crumbs have turned golden.

3 Add parsley, followed by the cooked pasta. Thin the sauce with a splash of pasta water, if needed.

4 Garnish with grated pecorino, to taste.

Substitution Tip Grated Parmesan can be substituted for the pecorino.
Storage Instructions Not optimal for leftovers, as the bread crumbs will soften in the oil mixture.

Aglio e Olio with Kale

SERVES 4

PREP TIME: 5 MIN
COOK TIME: 15 MIN

FLAVOR NOTE:
SPICY

VEGAN (OPTION), GLUTEN FREE, ONE POT, NUT FREE, 5 INGREDIENTS OR LESS, 30 MIN OR LESS

8 tablespoons extra-virgin olive oil

2 teaspoons red pepper flakes

4 cloves garlic, minced

3 cups chopped kale

½ teaspoon kosher salt

Parmesan, grated, for garnish (optional)

Aglio e Olio is Italian for "garlic and oil." It's a classic Italian pasta dish said to have originated from Naples. It's been around forever, and with good reason—it's incredibly delicious AND simple. I've decided to give this classic favorite a modern twist with the addition of chopped kale. Kale paired with the spicy red pepper flakes and garlicky pasta makes for a delizioso combination.

1   Heat the oil in a saucepan over medium heat. Add the pepper flakes and garlic, and cook until the garlic is fragrant, being careful not to burn it.

2   Add the kale and season with salt. Cook until wilted, stirring as necessary.

3   Add cooked pasta to pot and toss to coat.

4   Garnish with grated Parmesan, if desired.

Substitution Tip You could substitute spinach for kale.
Storage Instructions Transfer any leftovers to an airtight container and store in the refrigerator for up to 4 days.

White Clam Sauce with Chopped Walnuts

SERVES 4

PREP TIME: 15 MIN
COOK TIME: 15 MIN

FLAVOR NOTE:
SAVORY

ONE POT, 30 MIN OR LESS, GLUTEN FREE

6 tablespoons extra-virgin olive oil

¼ cup minced onion

6 cloves garlic, minced

1 cup dry white wine

24 littleneck clams, thoroughly cleaned

3 tablespoons unsalted butter

Juice of 1 lemon

3 tablespoons chopped parsley

1 tablespoon chopped walnuts

Tender littleneck clams steamed and bathed in a buttery garlic–white wine sauce and tossed with linguine—yum! It's the quintessential summertime seafood pasta dish. I've added a little something something—chopped walnuts—to give this classic a little extra texture and crunch. Don't let this restaurant favorite fool you; it's incredibly easy to recreate at home and much more friendly on the wallet when you do. Serve the remainder of the wine with the meal.

1 Heat the oil in a Dutch oven over medium heat. Add the onion and garlic and cook until softened, stirring as necessary.

2 Add the wine and allow it to reduce by half.

3 Add the clams, cover the pot with a lid, and cook until the clams have opened. (Note: Discard any clams that do not open after cooking.)

4 Once the clams have opened, add butter, lemon juice, and parsley.

5 Immediately add cooked pasta to the pot and toss to coat. Garnish with walnuts.

Time-Saving Tip You'll want to start your pasta at the same time you start making the sauce.

Storage Instructions Remove clam meat from shells and discard the shells prior to transferring any leftovers to an airtight container. Store in the refrigerator for up to 4 days.

Artichoke, Lemon, and Hazelnut Sauce

SERVES 4 TO 6

PREP TIME: 10 MIN

FLAVOR NOTES:
SAVORY, ZESTY

ONE POT, VEGETARIAN, GLUTEN FREE, GOOD FOR LEFTOVERS, MAKE AHEAD, 30 MIN OR LESS

¼ cup extra-virgin olive oil

1 tablespoon red wine vinegar

3 tablespoons lemon juice

1 tablespoon lemon zest

¼ teaspoon kosher salt

¼ teaspoon freshly ground black pepper

1 tablespoon sun-dried tomatoes (in olive oil), coarsely chopped

1 (12-ounce) jar artichoke hearts, drained, coarsely chopped

2 tablespoons hazelnuts, coarsely chopped

Parmesan, grated, for garnish

Pasta salads are perfect for picnics and potlucks because they're extremely versatile, and this one is no exception. This sauce boasts artichokes, lemon, and hazelnuts, and the pasta salad can be prepared in advance. If you're lucky enough to have any left, take it to work for lunch the next day. It even comes together quickly, because I've taken a shortcut by using prepared artichoke hearts.

1 In a large serving bowl, whisk together the olive oil, vinegar, lemon juice, and lemon zest. Season with salt and pepper.

2 Add the sun-dried tomatoes, artichoke hearts, and hazelnuts. Stir to combine.

3 Toss pasta with sauce then grate desired amount of Parmesan on top.

Serving Tip Try serving this pasta salad hot or cold.

Storage Instructions Transfer any leftovers to an airtight container and store in the refrigerator for up to 4 days.

Spicy Zucchini and Leek Sauce

SERVES 4 TO 6

PREP TIME: 10 MIN
COOK TIME: 20 MIN

FLAVOR NOTE:
SPICY

**VEGETARIAN, NUT FREE,
GLUTEN FREE, ONE POT,
30 MIN OR LESS**

½ cup extra-virgin olive oil, divided

1 large leek (white and light green portion only), thinly sliced

½ teaspoon red pepper flakes

2 cloves garlic, crushed

½ teaspoon kosher salt, divided

¼ cup dry white wine

1 large grated zucchini

¼ teaspoon lemon zest

Parmesan cheese, grated, for garnish

This spicy sauce is chock-full of green goodness and is perfect to serve all spring and summer long, especially if you have a garden overgrown with zucchini. Fragrant leeks are sautéed with garlic and a smidge of red pepper flakes for an extra punch of flavor, while the grated zucchini gives this dish a light feel. Serve with orecchiette (translates to "little ears" in Italian) pasta, which holds the sauce beautifully.

1 Heat ¼ cup olive oil in a saucepan over medium heat. Add the leek, red pepper flakes, and garlic. Season with ¼ teaspoon kosher salt and stir to combine. Cook until the leeks have softened, approximately 5 minutes.

2 Add the wine and allow it to reduce by half.

3 Add the zucchini and season with remaining kosher salt and lemon zest. Stir to combine and cook until the zucchini is heated through.

4 Taste for seasoning and add additional salt, if necessary. Discard the garlic cloves.

5 Finish by drizzling the remaining ¼ cup of olive oil into the sauce. Stir to combine. Garnish with grated Parmesan, to taste.

Option Tip Enjoy some of the leftover white wine with dinner.
Storage Instructions Transfer any leftovers to an airtight container and store in the refrigerator for up to 4 days.

Blender Curried Chickpea Sauce

SERVES 4

PREP TIME: 15 MIN
COOK TIME: 15 MIN

FLAVOR NOTE:
SPICY

**GLUTEN FREE, 5-INGREDIENT,
MAKE AHEAD, DAIRY FREE,
NUT FREE, 30 MIN OR LESS**

3 tablespoons extra-virgin olive oil

¼ cup minced onion

2 cloves garlic, peeled and crushed

3 teaspoons curry powder

1 (15-ounce) can chickpeas, drained

2 cups chicken stock

1½ cups reserved pasta water

Special Equipment: Blender

If you're looking for a dish that screams "take a walk on the modern side," you've found it. At first glance, this dish appears to be a creamy cheese-based sauce, but it is not. As a matter of fact, it's dairy-free! After cooking with spices, chickpeas are blended to a thick, smooth, hummus-like consistency and then thinned with reserved pasta water. The sauce is tossed with short pasta and is meant to be enjoyed immediately.

1   In a saucepan, heat the olive oil over medium heat. Add the onion and garlic, sautéing until fragrant. Be careful not to let the garlic burn. Stir as necessary.

2   Add the curry powder and chickpeas. Stir until coated. Add the chicken stock and bring to a slow boil. Cook until the chickpeas are tender.

3   Carefully transfer the mixture to your blender. Secure the lid, placing a kitchen towel on top for good measure. Blend until smooth.

4   The mixture will be thick, so add 1½ cups of reserved pasta water. Mix well.

Ingredient Tip Finish dish with a drizzle of chili oil for extra spice and a little extra kick.
Storage Instructions Transfer leftovers to an airtight container and store in the refrigerator for up to 4 days.

Fried Sage-Olive Oil Sauce with Crispy Prosciutto

SERVES 4

PREP TIME: 5 MIN
COOK TIME: 10 MIN

FLAVOR NOTE:
SAVORY

**NUT FREE, ONE POT,
VEGAN (OPTION), 30 MIN OR LESS,
GLUTEN FREE, DAIRY FREE**

6 tablespoons extra-virgin
   olive oil, divided

6 sage leaves

2 slices prosciutto, roughly torn

2 cloves garlic, crushed

Freshly ground black
   pepper, for garnish

In less time than it takes to cook pasta, you can have this Fried Sage-Olive Oil Sauce with Crispy Prosciutto ready. It begs to be paired with filled pasta, like tortellini or ravioli. Both the sage and prosciutto impart flavor into the olive oil and add a nice crispy texture to the final dish. It's perfect as a light lunch or as a dinner side dish. For a vegetarian or vegan option, simply omit the prosciutto.

1   Heat the olive oil in a saucepan over medium heat. Add the sage leaves and allow them to fry for 8 to 10 seconds, then carefully remove them using a slotted spoon. Transfer to a plate lined with paper towels or napkins to drain.

2   In the same saucepan, add the prosciutto and cook until crispy. Using a slotted spoon, carefully remove the prosciutto and transfer to a plate lined with paper towels or napkins to drain.

3   Add the garlic to the oil and cook until softened enough to smash with a fork. Continue pressing until it dissolves into the oil.

4   Immediately add your cooked pasta to the saucepan. Toss to coat. Sprinkle prosciutto and sage leaves on top. Season with freshly ground black pepper, to taste.

Time-Saving Tip Start cooking your pasta as soon as you begin preparing the sauce.

Storage Instructions Transfer any leftovers to an airtight container and store in the refrigerator for up to 4 days.

CHAPTER 3

TOMATO

WHEN YOU THINK OF ITALIAN PASTA sauces, chances are the first one that comes to mind would be a tomato-based sauce like the classic marinara. We really can't talk about sauces without talking tomatoes. The iconic fruit comes in many shapes, sizes, and forms. Did you know that there are over 15,000 varieties of tomatoes in the world? That is a lot of tomatoes. While there are many, the most familiar to Italian cooking are the San Marzano (the godfather of Italian tomatoes), Roma, and Ciliegino (cherry).

The tomato is so versatile that it can be incorporated into any meal—whether it's breakfast, lunch, or dinner. It can be eaten raw, turned into sauce, stuffed, stewed, etc.

You may be surprised to know that tomatoes arrived in Italy in the 16th century. However, tomatoes didn't make their way into kitchens until a few hundred years later. Originally, people thought the fruit might be poisonous and so it was used solely as an ornamental plant in gardens. Thankfully, some brave soul tasted it, lived to tell the tale, and now the tomato is considered to be one of the essential ingredients in southern Italian cooking. For this, we are all very grateful. Not only do they grow the majority of Italy's tomatoes in southern Italy, they export a great deal to the rest of the world as well.

As far back as I can remember, my parents always had a garden. They grew many varieties of fruits and vegetables, but their largest crop was tomatoes—more tomato plants than you could shake a stick at (as they say here in the South). Momma also preserved our harvest by canning our tomatoes so we could enjoy them year-round. We would have a garage full of mason jars—tomatoes in every form: whole, peeled, puréed, tomatoes with basil, crushed tomatoes, diced tomatoes. Every year, I didn't think it would be possible to make our way through hundreds of jars of those tomatoes, but somehow, we did. I miss having those jars. To me, the best fruits and vegetables are the ones you grow yourself. I am forever grateful to have had the love of growing fruits and vegetables instilled in me from an early age. Now, I have my own large container garden where I grow cherry tomatoes, fresh herbs, and peppers.

No garden? No problem. Farmers' markets are a wonderful place to shop for fresh tomatoes when they are in season, as well as your local grocery store. When tomatoes are not in season, there are many wonderful canned tomatoes available.

In this chapter, I'll give you ten tomato sauces for every season, including a Raw Summer Tomato Sauce (page 33) made with cherry tomatoes, a modern twist on the classic marinara with my Spicy Chipotle Tomato Sauce (page 31), and my Tomato Butternut Squash Sauce with Fried Sage Leaves (page 39). 🍅

Anchovy Tomato Sauce

SERVES 6

PREP TIME: 5 MIN
COOK TIME: 20 MIN

FLAVOR NOTES:
SAVORY, RICH, SALTY

**ONE POT, 30 MIN OR LESS,
GLUTEN FREE, NUT FREE**

3 tablespoons extra-virgin olive oil

¼ cup minced onion

2 cloves garlic, minced

½ teaspoon anchovy paste

14½ ounces diced tomatoes

1 teaspoon granulated sugar

¼ teaspoon kosher salt

⅛ teaspoon freshly ground
   black pepper

1 tablespoon unsalted butter

2 basil leaves

Anchovies add a salty, savory umami element to cooking. Anchovies are not as overpowering as one might think—they melt right into the sauce and give it that something extra that tickles the taste buds. I've taken a shortcut in this recipe and used anchovy paste, which is a nice way to ease into cooking with anchovies. Pair this savory sauce with spaghetti or tagliatelle.

1   Heat the olive oil in a heavy-bottomed saucepan over medium heat. Add the onion and garlic and sauté until softened, being careful not to let the garlic burn. Stir as necessary.

2   Add the anchovy paste and cook until incorporated.

3   Add the tomatoes and sugar and season with salt and pepper. Stir to combine. Reduce to a simmer and cook for about 10 minutes.

4   Add the butter and basil and stir to combine.

Ingredient Tip You can substitute whole anchovy fillets for anchovy paste. Allow them to cook until the fillets have melted into the sauce.

Storage Instructions Store leftovers in an airtight container in the refrigerator for up to 4 days.

Spicy Chipotle Tomato Sauce

SERVES 6

PREP TIME: 5 MIN
COOK TIME: 20 MIN

FLAVOR NOTE:
SPICY

**ONE POT, 5-INGREDIENT,
VEGETARIAN, GLUTEN FREE,
30 MIN OR LESS, NUT FREE**

2 tablespoons extra-virgin olive oil

¼ onion, minced

14½ ounces diced tomatoes

1 (8-ounce) can tomato sauce

¼ teaspoon kosher salt

⅛ teaspoon freshly ground
  black pepper

¼ teaspoon ground chipotle pepper

1 tablespoon unsalted butter

Because spice is nice, Spicy Chipotle Tomato Sauce is a fusion sauce that will light up your senses in the best possible way. The spicy element is brought to this sauce with the bold, earthy-smoky flavor of ground chipotle pepper. If you like your spice on the stronger side, increase the chipotle pepper to ½ teaspoon. This isn't a burning spice that will bring tears to your eyes. It just brings a little heat to the dish.

1 Heat oil in a heavy-bottomed saucepan over medium heat. Add the onion and cook until softened.

2 Add the tomatoes and season with salt, pepper, and chipotle pepper. Stir to combine and simmer for about 10 minutes.

3 Add the butter and stir to combine.

Option Tip For a smoother consistency, use an immersion blender or regular blender to purée the sauce once it has finished cooking.
Storage Instructions Store leftovers in an airtight container in the refrigerator for up to 4 days.

Blender Creamy Tomato Sauce with Goat Cheese

SERVES 6

PREP TIME: 5 MIN
COOK TIME: 5 MIN

FLAVOR NOTES:
RICH, TANGY, CREAMY

5 INGREDIENTS OR LESS, GLUTEN FREE, VEGETARIAN, MAKE AHEAD, GOOD FOR LEFTOVERS, 30 MIN OR LESS, NUT FREE

14½ ounces diced tomatoes

2 tablespoons goat cheese

½ teaspoon kosher salt

⅛ teaspoon freshly ground black pepper

2 basil leaves

Special Equipment: Blender

Looking for a no-fuss, no-frills, full-of-flavor pasta sauce? Then this Blender Creamy Tomato Sauce with Goat Cheese is perfect for you. If you happen to have a blender with a heating function, you can make the sauce entirely in your blender. If not, pour it into a saucepan after blending and warm through. By the time your pasta is ready, the sauce will be, too. I like to pair this easy-peasy sauce with bucatini.

1 Add the tomatoes, goat cheese, salt, and pepper into your blender and blend until smooth.

2 Transfer to a heavy-bottomed saucepan. Add the basil and heat over medium heat until warmed through.

Option Tip To take the dish over the top, sprinkle it with additional crumbled goat cheese.

Storage Instructions Store leftovers in an airtight container in the refrigerator for up to 4 days.

Raw Summer Tomato Sauce

SERVES 4

PREP TIME: 5 MIN

FLAVOR NOTE:
TANGY

**MAKE AHEAD, GOOD FOR
LEFTOVERS, VEGETARIAN,
5 INGREDIENTS OR LESS,
30 MIN OR LESS, GLUTEN FREE,
NUT FREE**

1 pint cherry tomatoes, halved

1 clove garlic, minced

3 tablespoons extra-virgin olive oil

½ teaspoon kosher salt

¼ teaspoon freshly ground
  black pepper

4 ounces mozzarella pearls

3 basil leaves, chiffonade cut

*This is the perfect sauce to have in your summertime
recipe repertoire, when cherry tomatoes are plentiful and
extra sweet and when you don't want to heat up the
kitchen. It's a no-cook, 5-minute, make-ahead pasta salad
sauce (with no mayo) that is perfect for picnics, potlucks,
and light lunches all summer long. This sauce can be
served at room temperature or chilled. Pair with short
pasta—like farfalle, orecchiette, or penne—and consider
finishing it off with a drizzle of balsamic glaze.*

1   In a large bowl, combine the tomatoes, garlic, and olive oil.
    Season with salt and pepper.
2   Add the mozzarella pearls and stir to combine.
3   Garnish with basil leaves.

Ingredient Tip *Chiffonade* is a culinary term meaning to slice into thin
ribbons. The easiest way to achieve this is to stack the basil leaves together,
roll them, and then slice them thinly.
Storage Instructions Store leftovers in an airtight container in the refrigerator for up to 4 days.

Red Clam Sauce with Crispy Pancetta

SERVES 4

PREP TIME: 10 MIN
COOK TIME: 20 MIN

FLAVOR NOTES:
SAVORY, BRINY

**ONE POT, 30 MIN OR LESS,
GLUTEN FREE, NUT FREE**

8 ounces pancetta, diced

4 tablespoons extra-virgin olive oil

¼ cup minced onion

6 cloves garlic, minced

1 cup dry white wine

¼ teaspoon kosher salt

24 littleneck clams,
  thoroughly cleaned

1 cup crushed tomatoes

3 tablespoons unsalted butter

Juice of 1 lemon

3 tablespoons chopped parsley

If you've only ever ordered linguine and clams at a restaurant because you thought it would be too difficult to recreate, I'm here to tell you that you absolutely can make this easily at home. This would make a great dinner for date night at home, served with the remaining wine—and don't forget to grab a baguette to soak up all that sensational sauce! It's also easy and elegant enough for a small dinner party.

1   Sauté the pancetta in a Dutch oven over medium heat until crisp, approximately 4 or 5 minutes. Transfer to a paper towel–lined plate, then remove all but 1 tablespoon of the grease left behind.

2   Add the olive oil and return to medium heat. Add the onion and garlic and cook until softened, stirring as necessary.

3   Add the wine and allow the mixture to reduce by half. Season with salt.

4   Add the clams. Cover the pot with a lid and cook until the clams have opened. (Note: Discard any clams that do not open after cooking.)

5   Once clams have opened, add the tomatoes, butter, lemon juice, and parsley.

6   Immediately add cooked pasta to pot and toss to combine. Garnish with crispy pancetta.

Time-Saving Tip You'll want to start your pasta at the same time you start making the sauce.
Storage Instructions Remove the clam meat from the shells and discard the shells before storing. Transfer any leftovers to an airtight container and store in the refrigerator for up to 4 days.

Summer Vegetable Chunky Marinara

SERVES 6

PREP TIME: 5 MIN
COOK TIME: 25 MIN

FLAVOR NOTE:
SAVORY

**ONE POT, VEGETARIAN,
GLUTEN FREE, 30 MIN OR LESS,
NUT FREE**

2 tablespoons extra-virgin olive oil

¼ onion, minced

2 cloves garlic, minced

1 zucchini, diced

1 crookneck (yellow) squash, diced

½ teaspoon kosher salt, divided

¼ teaspoon freshly ground
  black pepper, divided

14½ ounces diced tomatoes

1 (8-ounce) can tomato sauce

2 tablespoons unsalted butter

2 or 3 basil leaves

When the summer vegetable harvest is in overdrive, it's the perfect time to create a chunky marinara sauce. Zucchini and summer squash (yellow or crookneck) are diced and sautéed with onion and garlic until soft, then they're bathed in tomatoes and simmered slowly until the flavors mingle, creating a summer cornucopia. This pairs well with farfalle and would be a delicious topper for chicken.

1 Heat the olive oil in a skillet over medium heat. Add the onion and garlic and sauté until softened, being careful not to let the garlic burn.

2 Add the zucchini and crookneck squash and season with salt and pepper. Cook until slightly softened.

3 Add tomatoes and tomato sauce. Season with remaining salt and pepper. Add the butter and basil and stir to combine. Reduce the heat to a simmer and cook for about 10 minutes, or until the vegetables are fork-tender.

Ingredient Tip Mushrooms would be a great earthy addition to this sauce.
Storage Instructions Store leftovers in an airtight container in the refrigerator for up to 4 days.

Roasted Fennel Tomato Sauce

SERVES 4

PREP TIME: 10 MIN
COOK TIME: 45 MIN

FLAVOR NOTE:
SAVORY

VEGETARIAN, NUT FREE

1 bulb fennel, fronds removed
   (save for garnish if desired), sliced

½ onion, sliced

4 cloves garlic, peeled

1 pint cherry tomatoes

3 or 4 tablespoons
   extra-virgin olive oil

½ teaspoon kosher salt

¼ teaspoon freshly ground
   black pepper

1½ cups crushed tomatoes

1 tablespoon unsalted butter

½ cup reserved pasta water

Special Equipment: Mandoline,
   if available

If you're not familiar with fennel, it has a body similar to an onion with stalks and leaves. It also has a very distinct licorice smell to it. When it's roasted, you don't pick up on the licorice. Instead, it takes on a sweet flavor that complements the tomatoes nicely.

1   Preheat your oven to 425°F.

2   Line a rimmed baking sheet with aluminum foil and spread the sliced fennel, onion, garlic, and cherry tomatoes out in a layer on the baking sheet. Season with salt and pepper and drizzle with just enough olive oil to coat.

3   Bake for approximately 30 minutes, or until all the vegetables are fork-tender.

4   Carefully transfer the contents, including liquid, into a saucepan. Add the crushed tomatoes and butter and stir to combine. Heat over medium heat until warmed through, stirring as necessary. Taste for seasoning, adding more salt and pepper if needed.

5   Add the reserved pasta water and stir to combine.

Tool Tip Using a mandoline to slice fennel and onion will give you even, consistent slices with little effort. If you don't own one, carefully slicing with a knife will work just as well.

Storage Instructions Transfer any leftovers to an airtight container and store in the refrigerator for up to 4 days.

Barolo Tomato Sauce

SERVES 6

PREP TIME: 5 MIN
COOK TIME: 30 MIN

FLAVOR NOTES:
SAVORY, RICH

**ONE POT, VEGETARIAN,
GLUTEN FREE, NUT FREE**

2 tablespoons extra-virgin olive oil

½ onion, minced

2 cloves garlic, minced

1 cup Barolo wine

14½ ounces diced tomatoes

1 (8-ounce) can tomato sauce

½ teaspoon kosher salt

¼ teaspoon freshly ground
  black pepper

2 or 3 basil leaves

1 (1-inch) section of Parmesan rind

Barolo is a full-bodied red wine that pairs beautifully with tomatoes. It adds an extra level of richness and depth to the sauce. This sauce pairs well with spaghetti and begs to be sprinkled with additional Parmesan. There will be plenty of wine left over from the recipe to enjoy with the meal.

1   Heat the olive oil in a heavy-bottomed saucepan over medium heat. Add the onion and garlic and sauté until softened, stirring as necessary and being careful not to burn the garlic.

2   Add the wine and allow the liquid to reduce by half.

3   Add the tomatoes and tomato sauce. Season with salt and pepper and stir to combine.

4   Add the basil and Parmesan rind. Reduce the heat to a simmer and continue cooking for about 20 minutes, stirring as necessary.

Substitution Tip You can substitute a cabernet or other full-bodied red wine if Barolo isn't available.

Storage Instructions Store leftovers in an airtight container in the refrigerator for up to 4 days.

Hearty Cannellini Beans in Tomato Sauce

SERVES 4 TO 6

PREP TIME: 10 MIN
COOK TIME: 30 MIN

FLAVOR NOTE:
SAVORY

ONE POT, KID FRIENDLY, VEGETARIAN, GLUTEN FREE, NUT FREE

2 tablespoons extra-virgin olive oil

¼ onion, minced

2 cloves garlic, minced

14½ ounces diced tomatoes

1 (8-ounce) can tomato sauce

2 or 3 basil leaves

1 (15½-ounce) can cannellini
  beans, drained

½ teaspoon kosher salt

¼ teaspoon freshly ground
  black pepper

1 roasted red bell pepper, diced

2 tablespoons unsalted butter

½ cup dry white wine

Cannellini beans (often referred to as white beans) are kidney-shaped, creamy beans. They add a stick-to-your-ribs element to this dish that pairs beautifully with the tomatoes, and they are slowly simmered until the flavors meld together. Pair it with penne and a nicely cooked chicken breast for a complete meal. It's pure comfort food in a bowl.

1   Heat the olive oil in a heavy-bottomed saucepan over medium heat. Add the onion and garlic and sauté until softened, stirring as necessary and being careful not to burn the garlic.

2   Add the tomatoes, tomato sauce, basil, and beans. Season with salt and pepper and stir to combine.

3   Add the roasted red bell pepper, butter, and wine. Stir to combine. Reduce the heat to low and simmer for about 15 minutes.

Option Tip This sauce is thick and hearty enough that it can also be used as a side dish. Cut a few slices of your favorite baguette and dip away.

Storage Instructions Store leftovers in an airtight container in the refrigerator for up to 4 days.

Tomato Butternut Squash Sauce with Fried Sage Leaves

SERVES 4 TO 6

PREP TIME: 15 MIN
COOK TIME: 45 MIN

FLAVOR NOTE:
SAVORY

VEGETARIAN, MAKE AHEAD, KID FRIENDLY, NUT FREE

1 small butternut squash, peeled, halved, seeded, and cubed

3 or 4 tablespoons extra-virgin olive oil, divided

½ teaspoon kosher salt

¼ teaspoon freshly ground black pepper

½ teaspoon ground cumin

4 to 6 sage leaves

¼ cup minced onion

2 cloves garlic, minced

1 cup crushed tomatoes

½ cup reserved pasta water

This is a winter sauce recipe that uses an unexpected ingredient—roasted butternut squash. The squash is peeled, cubed, seasoned with cumin, and roasted until fork-tender. When combined with the crushed tomatoes, it adds a creamy element to this rich sauce. Pair this savory sauce with rigatoni.

1   Preheat your oven to 425°F.

2   Line a rimmed baking sheet with aluminum foil and spread the cubed squash out in a single layer. Drizzle with 2 or 3 tablespoons olive oil and sprinkle with salt, pepper, and cumin. Toss to coat.

3   Bake for about 25 minutes, or until fork-tender.

4   Heat 1 tablespoon olive oil in a saucepan over medium heat. When the oil is hot, add the sage leaves and allow to fry for 8 to 10 seconds. Using a slotted spoon, transfer the sage leaves to a plate lined with a paper towel.

5   Add the onion and garlic to the oil. Sauté until softened, stirring as necessary and being careful not to let the garlic burn.

6   Add the tomatoes and stir to combine. Season with salt and pepper.

7   Add the roasted squash, smashing the squash with a large wooden spoon or a potato masher. Stir to combine.

8   Thin the sauce with the reserved pasta water until it reaches the desired consistency.

Time-Saving Tip The squash can be roasted in advance to save time.
Storage Instructions Transfer any leftovers to an airtight container and store in the refrigerator for up to 4 days.

CHAPTER 4

CREAM

ALTHOUGH I'VE NEVER MET A SAUCE I DIDN'T like, I have a soft spot for cream sauces. There are so many varieties of cream: clotted cream, crème fraîche, whipping cream, sour cream, heavy cream, half-and-half, double cream . . .

'm of the opinion that if you're going to use cream, you might as well use heavy cream. All the recipes in this chapter are made using heavy whipping cream. Heavy whipping cream is simply the thick part of the milk that rises to the top due to its high fat content. It's rich, creamy, and decadent: everything you want in a cream sauce.

One of my favorite cream sauces is the one my momma would make. It also happens to be the easiest. She learned the recipe in one of the many cooking classes she attended while we were living in northern Italy and of course passed it on to me. It was simply referred to as a "white sauce," and it's a combination of only three ingredients that you may already have in your refrigerator. It is mind-blowingly delicious, takes minutes to make, and pairs well with everything from spaghetti to filled pasta like tortellini. Look for my White Sauce with Crispy Bacon Crumbles (page 44) for a twist on this famous-to-me sauce. It's one you'll be coming back to more often than not.

There are a few things to know when cooking with cream, like how to prevent it from curdling. No one wants that. Trust me. First and most important, don't let the cream boil. Go with a gentle medium-low heat. Wait until the end of cooking to season your sauce as well.

I've included cream recipes that vary, from my take on the traditional white sauce to a creamy cauliflower sauce that will have you rethinking cauliflower, and even an avocado (yes, avocado) cream sauce that you may want to eat with a spoon.

There are artichokes, roasted carrots, and even a Roasted Garlic Blender Sauce (page 49) that will have you questioning why you don't keep roasted garlic heads in the kitchen on a regular basis. You may want to grab some breath mints for that one, but it's completely worth it. One thing to note when using a blender with a cream-based sauce is we do not want to end up with whipped cream. Save that for desserts. The pulse button on the blender is your friend. If you blend too quickly, you will end up with—you guessed it—whipped cream. Slow and steady. If, by chance, it becomes too thick, you can thin it out with a little reserved pasta water. That water is magical.

There are 10 very different cream-based recipes in this chapter, and I'm certain you'll find at least one, if not several, that piques your interest. Love mushrooms? How could I do a cream-based chapter and not include one? I have you covered with a Mushroom-Herb Sauce (page 50). Spinach your preference? Awesome. You'll want to look for my Creamy Spinach-Parm Sauce (page 52).

There is something for everyone here in these 10 creamy, dreamy pasta sauces. All that you'll need to decide on is which pasta to pair your favorite recipe with. 🍎

White Sauce with Crispy Bacon Crumbles

SERVES 4

PREP TIME: 5 MIN
COOK TIME: 10 MIN

FLAVOR NOTE:
SAVORY, RICH, CREAMY

**KID FRIENDLY, 5 INGREDIENTS
OR LESS, VEGETARIAN (OPTION),
GLUTEN FREE, NUT FREE,
30 MIN OR LESS**

2 or 3 strips thick-cut bacon, diced

½ cup sour cream

1 cup heavy whipping cream

1 cup grated Parmesan

½ teaspoon kosher salt

¼ teaspoon freshly ground
   black pepper

This is a one-size-fits-all, quick and simple white sauce that pairs well with any pasta type (including filled pasta). It's made using just three ingredients that you may already have on hand, plus a little salt and pepper. Once the sauce is paired with pasta, we've topped the dish with crispy bacon crumbles—because, let's face it, bacon makes everything better.

1   Place the bacon into a 3.5- or 5-quart Dutch oven over medium heat and cook until the bacon is crispy. Remove with a slotted spoon and transfer to a plate lined with paper towels or napkins. Wipe the pan clean.

2   In the clean Dutch oven, add the sour cream, whipping cream, and Parmesan. Whisk to combine and season with salt and pepper. Heat over medium-low heat until the mixture slightly thickens, stirring as necessary. Be careful not to let the sauce boil, as the cream could curdle.

Substitution Tip Omit the bacon crumbles for a vegetarian option.
Storage Instructions Transfer any leftovers to an airtight container and store in the refrigerator for up to 4 days.

Creamy Cauliflower Sauce

SERVES 4 TO 6

PREP TIME: 5 MIN
COOK TIME: 20 MIN

FLAVOR NOTE:
SAVORY, RICH, CREAMY

**VEGETARIAN, KID FRIENDLY,
5-INGREDIENT, 30 MIN OR LESS,
NUT FREE, GLUTEN FREE,**

1 head cauliflower, trimmed, stems
   discarded (about 4 cups cooked)
½ cup heavy whipping cream
3 tablespoons unsalted butter
2 cloves garlic, minced
½ teaspoon kosher salt
¼ teaspoon freshly ground
   black pepper
½ cup grated Parmesan

Special Equipment: Blender

Cauliflower is the current undisputed "it girl" of vegetables. It magically transforms to be used in a wide variety of recipes, including in this rich and silky white sauce. Cauliflower florets are boiled until fork-tender, transferred to a blender, and puréed with cream until smooth. A quick trip back into the Dutch oven with a few additional ingredients, and you're on your way to enjoying this creamy cauliflower goodness.

1 Fill a 3.5- or 5-quart Dutch oven halfway with water and bring to a boil. Add the cauliflower florets and cook until fork-tender. Drain, discarding the water.

2 Transfer the cooked cauliflower to a blender. Add the heavy whipping cream and pulse until smooth.

3 In the Dutch oven, melt the butter over medium heat. Add the garlic and cook until fragrant, stirring frequently and being careful not to let the garlic burn.

4 Return the cauliflower mixture to the Dutch oven and season with salt and pepper. Stir to combine. Cook until warmed through, stirring as necessary.

Ingredient Tip If the mixture is too thick, thin it with a little reserved pasta water.
Storage Instructions Transfer any leftovers to an airtight container and store in the refrigerator for up to 4 days.

Avocado Cream Sauce

SERVES 4

PREP TIME: 10 MIN
COOK TIME: 5 MIN

FLAVOR NOTE:
SAVORY, RICH, CREAMY

**5-INGREDIENT, VEGETARIAN,
30 MIN OR LESS, GLUTEN FREE,
NUT FREE**

2 or 3 ripe avocados
 (2 large or 3 small or medium),
 halved and pitted

1 teaspoon fresh lemon juice

½ cup heavy whipping cream

½ teaspoon kosher salt

¼ teaspoon freshly ground
 black pepper

1 tablespoon extra-virgin olive oil

2 cloves garlic, minced

2 or 3 basil leaves, chiffonade
 cut, for garnish

*Avocados aren't just for guacamole or avocado toast—
they're surprisingly versatile. With them, you can make
an incredibly rich and creamy sauce that's perfect for any
short or long pasta of your choosing. Also note, because of
the browning nature of avocados, this recipe isn't suited
for leftovers, so plan on eating it in one sitting.*

1   Scoop the avocado flesh from the skins and place into
    a medium bowl. Add the lemon juice and cream and
    mash together with a fork until smooth. Season with salt
    and pepper.

2   Heat the oil in a saucepan over medium heat. Add the garlic
    and sauté until fragrant.

3   Add the avocado mixture and heat until just warmed through.
    Stir until smooth.

4   Toss with desired pasta and garnish with basil.

Ingredient Tip Chiffonade is a culinary term meaning to slice into thin
ribbons. The easiest way to achieve this is to stack the basil leaves together,
roll them, and then slice them thinly.

Recipe Tip If the avocado sauce is too thick, thin it out using reserved
pasta water.

Storage Instructions Because of the browning nature of avocados, this
sauce does not keep well for leftovers.

Creamy Artichoke Sauce

SERVES 6

PREP TIME: 5 MIN
COOK TIME: 15 MIN

FLAVOR NOTE:
SAVORY, RICH, CREAMY

**VEGETARIAN, 30 MIN OR LESS,
GLUTEN FREE, NUT FREE,
GOOD FOR LEFTOVERS**

2 tablespoons unsalted butter

1 tablespoon extra-virgin olive oil

2 cloves garlic, minced

1 (12-ounce) jar artichoke
  hearts, drained and chopped

½ teaspoon kosher salt

¼ teaspoon freshly ground
  black pepper

¾ cup heavy whipping cream

¼ to ½ cup grated Parmesan

¼ teaspoon fresh lemon
  juice, for serving

Special Equipment: Blender

If you want a rich, creamy, quick, and delicious artichoke sauce, this is the one. It's a perfect weeknight dinner candidate. I realize a whole globe artichoke can be intimidating, but there's no need to worry. We're taking a shortcut and using jarred artichoke hearts. Once the sauce is heated through, you'll simply blend everything to a smooth consistency. Bonus: it makes wonderful leftovers.

1 Heat the butter and oil in a heavy-bottomed saucepan over medium heat. Add the garlic and cook until fragrant, stirring as necessary and being careful not to let the garlic burn.

2 Add the artichoke hearts, salt, pepper, cream, and Parmesan. Cook just until mixture has warmed through.

3 Transfer the mixture to blender (or use an immersion blender) and pulse just until smooth. Be careful not to overmix or the mixture will be too thick.

4 Finish with a drizzle of lemon juice.

Ingredient Tip Pair this sauce with your favorite short, stocky pasta.
Storage Instructions Transfer any leftovers to an airtight container and store in the refrigerator for up to 4 days.

Creamy Roasted Carrot Sauce

SERVES 4

PREP TIME: 10 MIN
COOK TIME: 35 MIN

FLAVOR NOTE:
SAVORY, CREAMY

**KID FRIENDLY, VEGETARIAN
(OPTION), GLUTEN FREE,
NUT FREE**

1 pound carrots, peeled

¼ onion, sliced

3 tablespoons extra-virgin olive oil

½ teaspoon kosher salt

¼ teaspoon freshly ground
black pepper

¾ to 1 cup chicken stock, divided

½ teaspoon garlic paste

¾ cup heavy whipping cream

Fresh thyme, for garnish

Special Equipment: Blender

I haven't met a vegetable that I didn't love roasted, and carrots are no exception. When they are roasted, they achieve this slightly sweet flavor and have a beautifully caramelized exterior. Once roasted, the carrots and onion are blended into a smooth sauce that has a naturally vibrant color. This sauce pairs well with any short, stocky pasta. For a twist, try tossing it with gnocchi.

1   Preheat oven to 400°F.

2   Place the carrots and onion onto a rimmed baking sheet. Drizzle with olive oil and season with salt and pepper. Stir to coat. Bake for about 30 minutes, or until fork-tender.

3   Transfer cooked carrots to the blender. Add chicken stock ¼ cup at a time and blend until smooth. The amount of stock necessary will depend on the size of the carrots.

4   Add the remaining chicken stock and garlic paste to a heavy-bottomed saucepan over medium heat. Add the blended carrots and onion and cream and stir to combine. Cook until just warmed through. Taste for seasoning. If necessary, add additional salt and pepper to taste.

5   Toss with pasta and garnish with thyme.

Time-Saving Tip You could easily roast a tray of vegetables in advance while you have the oven on for another meal.
Storage Instructions Transfer any leftovers to an airtight container and store in the refrigerator for up to 4 days.
Substitution Tip You could easily make this sauce vegetarian by swapping the chicken stock for vegetable stock.

Roasted Garlic Blender Sauce

SERVES 4

PREP TIME: 5 MIN
COOK TIME: 35 MIN

FLAVOR NOTE:
SAVORY

VEGETARIAN, 5 INGREDIENTS OR LESS, GLUTEN FREE, NUT FREE

1 head garlic, top removed

1 tablespoon extra-virgin olive oil

1½ cups heavy whipping cream

1 cup grated Parmesan

½ teaspoon kosher salt

¼ teaspoon freshly ground black pepper

Special Equipment: Blender

Roasted garlic is incredibly easy to make and fantastic to have on hand. There is no need to peel the garlic head before roasting—you'll simply slice off enough of the top of the garlic head to expose the cloves. When it's time to blend, remember to pulse only enough to combine the ingredients; otherwise, you may end up with whipped cream.

1 Preheat oven to 400°F.

2 Place the garlic onto a sheet of aluminum foil big enough to surround the entire head. Drizzle the top with olive oil, then wrap the foil loosely around the head. Bake for approximately 30 minutes, or until the garlic is lightly browned and softened.

3 Remove the garlic cloves from the peels and transfer the cloves to the blender. Add the cream, Parmesan, salt, and pepper and pulse just until the garlic is incorporated. Be careful not to over-blend.

4 Pour the garlic mixture into a heavy-bottomed saucepan. Heat on low until just warmed through.

Time-Saving Tip While you already have the oven on, consider doubling the recipe to use leftover roasted garlic for other recipes.
Storage Instructions Transfer any leftovers to an airtight container and store in the refrigerator for up to 4 days.

Mushroom-Herb Sauce

SERVES 4

PREP TIME: 5 MIN
COOK TIME: 20 MIN

FLAVOR NOTES:
SAVORY, RICH

**VEGETARIAN KID FRIENDLY,
30 MIN OR LESS, GLUTEN FREE,
NUT FREE**

3 tablespoons unsalted butter

3 cloves garlic, minced

8 ounces baby bella
    mushrooms, sliced

½ teaspoon kosher salt

¼ teaspoon freshly ground
    black pepper

1 tablespoon all-purpose flour

1 cup heavy whipping cream

2 or 3 sprigs of fresh
    thyme, for garnish

If you're a fan of cream of mushroom soup, this is the equivalent in sauce form. The mushrooms are sautéed in butter until they're beautifully browned. A light sprinkling of flour is added to help the sauce thicken and then the cream comes into play, mixing with the mushrooms to form a rich and decadent sauce. If you're so inclined, sprinkle fresh Parmesan or pecorino cheese on top.

1   Heat the butter in a 3.5- or 5-quart Dutch oven over medium heat. Add the garlic and sauté until fragrant, being careful not to burn the garlic.

2   Add the mushrooms and season with salt and pepper. Cook until the mushrooms have softened, released their natural water, and started to brown. Stir as necessary.

3   Add the flour, stirring so that the mushrooms are lightly coated. Add the cream and reduce the heat to low. Simmer until the sauce thickens.

4   Taste for seasoning, adding salt and pepper to taste, if necessary. Garnish with thyme.

Ingredient Tip Pair this sauce with a flat noodle, such as tagliatelle.
Storage Instructions Transfer any leftovers to an airtight container and store in the refrigerator for up to 4 days.

Lemon-Basil Ricotta Cheese Sauce

SERVES 4 TO 6

PREP TIME: 5 MIN
COOK TIME: 5 MIN

FLAVOR NOTES:
SAVORY, ZESTY

**VEGETARIAN, 5-INGREDIENT,
KID FRIENDLY, 30 MIN OR LESS,
GLUTEN FREE, NUT FREE**

1 tablespoon extra-virgin olive oil

½ teaspoon garlic paste

¾ cup ricotta cheese

1 cup heavy whipping cream

¼ teaspoon lemon zest

½ teaspoon kosher salt

¼ teaspoon freshly ground
  black pepper

3 basil leaves

*Short on time? No problem. This is a 5-ingredient,
5-minute sauce. Lemon-Basil Ricotta Cheese Sauce is
light and bright and comes together in less time than it
takes to boil your pasta. It pairs well with fusilli or even
filled pastas. The ricotta cheese blends beautifully with
the lemon and basil in this recipe. Garnish the sauce with
extra freshly ground black pepper and lemon zest.*

1 Heat the oil in a heavy-bottomed saucepan over medium
   heat. Add the garlic paste, ricotta, cream, and lemon zest. Stir
   to combine and season with salt and pepper.

2 Reduce the heat to a simmer before adding the basil, and
   cook until the sauce has slightly thickened and is warmed
   through. Stir as necessary.

Ingredient Tip Pair this sauce with tortellini or ravioli.
Storage Instructions Transfer any leftovers to an airtight container
and store in the refrigerator for up to 4 days.

Creamy Spinach-Parm Sauce

SERVES 4

PREP TIME: 5 MIN
COOK TIME: 15 MIN

FLAVOR NOTES:
SAVORY, CREAMY, RICH

**VEGETARIAN, KID FRIENDLY,
30 MIN OR LESS, GLUTEN FREE,
NUT FREE**

1 tablespoon unsalted butter

1 tablespoon extra-virgin olive oil

½ teaspoon garlic paste

¼ onion, minced

4 ounces fresh baby spinach

½ teaspoon kosher salt

¼ teaspoon freshly ground
  black pepper

1 cup heavy whipping cream

¼ cup grated Parmesan

Creamed spinach is one of my favorite side dishes, and whenever I can pair spinach with cream, I usually do. I've always been amazed how the spinach will look like it's taking over the entire saucepan but will magically wilt in a minute. Once it's wilted, it mixes with the cream and cheese to create a balanced sauce. Serve with spaghetti for a completely vegetarian option, or, for carnivores, consider topping with grilled chicken breasts.

1   Heat the butter and oil in a heavy-bottomed saucepan over medium heat. Add the garlic paste and onion and sauté until fragrant.

2   Add the spinach and cook until wilted, stirring as necessary. Season with salt and pepper.

3   Add the cream and Parmesan and stir well to combine. Continue cooking until sauce slightly thickens and is warmed through.

Ingredient Tip Pair this sauce with spaghetti.
Storage Instructions Transfer any leftovers to an airtight container and store in the refrigerator for up to 4 days.

Creamy Sun-Dried Tomato Blender Sauce

SERVES 4

PREP TIME: 5 MIN
COOK TIME: 15 MIN

FLAVOR NOTES:
SAVORY, RICH, CREAMY

**KID FRIENDLY, VEGETARIAN,
5 INGREDIENTS OR LESS, 30 MIN
OR LESS, GLUTEN FREE, NUT FREE**

1 tablespoon extra-virgin olive oil

½ teaspoon garlic paste

2 tablespoons sun-dried tomatoes
  (oil-packed), chopped

1¼ cups heavy whipping cream

½ teaspoon kosher salt

¼ teaspoon freshly ground
  black pepper

¼ cup grated Parmesan

Special Equipment: Blender

Heavy cream is infused with sun-dried tomatoes to create a rich and silky sauce. It practically begs you to bring a slice of baguette to the plate to soak up every last drop. It also couldn't be easier to make. This is a 5-ingredient, 15-minute wonder sauce that's soon to be in your regular dinner rotation.

1 Heat the oil in a heavy-bottomed saucepan over medium heat. Add the garlic paste, sun-dried tomatoes, and cream. Season with salt and pepper and stir to combine.

2 Add the Parmesan and simmer until warmed through.

3 Transfer to a blender and pulse until smooth.

Ingredient Tip Pair this sauce with a thin pasta, like spaghetti.
Storage Instructions Transfer any leftovers to an airtight container and store in the refrigerator for up to 4 days.

CHAPTER 5

PESTO

PESTO IS A WONDERFULLY BRIGHT SAUCE that is as versatile as it is varied. Pesto can be used as a pasta sauce, a condiment, a spread for crackers or bread, a dip, a base for pizza, and on and on. The only limit is your imagination.

What exactly is pesto? Pesto is the past tense of *pestare*, which means "to crush" in Italian. When we think pesto, we typically think of the OG pesto: the beautiful green sauce *pesto alla Genovese*. It originated in Genoa, Italy, from where it derives its Genovese name. Pesto traditionally consists of garlic, European pine nuts, coarse salt, fresh basil leaves, and hard cheeses (such as Parmesan or pecorino) mixed together using a mortar and pestle and emulsified with olive oil. While I typically use a food processor, you could absolutely use a mortar and pestle if you have one handy.

Today, pestos are made using a variety of different nuts. In this chapter, we'll use pine nuts, cashews, pistachios, walnuts, and even pumpkin seeds. If you need a substitute for pine nuts, which tend to be expensive, you can consider using almonds.

One thing to consider is whether or not to toast nuts prior to using. If you have the time, it's always a good idea to do so. There are many ways to toast nuts, but the easiest way is to simply add nuts to a dry, unoiled skillet and allow them to toast over medium heat until they turn golden. Be careful not to burn them. Toasting is so simple and will add additional flavor and texture to your dishes.

In some recipes in this chapter, I've also swapped out traditional basil, opting for more out-of-the-box ingredients like kale, spinach, and arugula.

There are 10 very different versions of pesto in this chapter. I frequently turn to the Kale and Pistachio Pesto (page 62), because it's so bright and the flavors just pop. The Sun-Dried Tomato Pesto with Walnuts and Black Pepper (page 65) is incredibly delicious and develops over time, while the Preserved Lemon and Cashew Pesto (page 64) will definitely have lemon fans taking a second glance.

Each one of the recipes makes about half a cup. You can easily double the recipe if you need more. I prefer to store my pesto in small glass canning jars. I top off the jar with a thin layer of olive oil before storing in the refrigerator to help keep it fresh. 🍎

Roasted Beet Pesto

YIELDS ½ CUP

PREP TIME: 10 MIN
COOK TIME: 45 MIN

FLAVOR NOTE:
NUTTY

VEGETARIAN, 5 INGREDIENTS OR LESS, GLUTEN FREE

1 large beet, washed, top trimmed

½ cup extra-virgin olive oil, plus more for roasting

3 cloves garlic, peeled

½ cup pine nuts

½ cup grated Parmesan

¼ teaspoon kosher salt

Special Equipment: Food Processor

Beets are divisive: You either love them or you hate them. I happen to love them. When roasted, they take on a subtle, sweet flavor. They do require a little time to roast, so plan ahead. I advise you to wear gloves when handling beets to avoid staining your hands. Once roasted, everything goes into the food processor and voilà! *Roasted Beet Pesto.*

1 Preheat oven to 425°F.

2 Place the beet onto a piece of aluminum foil large enough to fold over and cover the beet. Drizzle with enough olive oil to lightly coat. Seal the foil around the beet and transfer to a rimmed baking sheet to bake for about 45 minutes, or until fork-tender.

3 When the beet is cool enough to handle, remove the skin and discard.

4 In a food processor, add the roasted beet and garlic. Pulse to combine. Add the nuts and Parmesan and pulse again to combine. Continue pulsing, carefully streaming the olive oil into the food processor as it runs, until the mixture is combined.

5 Add salt and stir to combine.

Option Tip To turn the pesto into a pasta sauce, place 2 tablespoons of pesto in the bottom of a single-serving dish and add a small drizzle of olive oil and a splash of reserved pasta water. Mix until it's smooth, add warm pasta, and toss to coat. The sauce should coat the pasta and not clump. You could also mix the pesto with vegetables using this method.

Storage Instructions Transfer to an airtight container and store in the refrigerator for up to 4 days.

Arugula and Mint Pesto

YIELDS ½ CUP

PREP TIME: 10 MIN

FLAVOR NOTES:
NUTTY, PEPPERY, SAVORY

VEGETARIAN, 30 MIN OR LESS, GLUTEN FREE

1 cup loosely packed arugula

1 cup loosely packed fresh mint

2 cloves garlic, peeled

⅓ cup cashews

⅓ cup grated Parmesan

⅓ cup extra-virgin olive oil

¼ teaspoon kosher salt

¼ teaspoon lemon juice

Special Equipment: Food Processor

This Arugula and Mint Pesto is a great way to add flavor to everything from meats to pasta. Arugula is peppery when mixed with mint and buttery cashews, and it creates a fantastic flavor profile. When combining the ingredients in the food processor, be sure they're mixed well after each pulse. If you prefer your pesto with a looser texture, simply add a little additional olive oil. Store your pesto in airtight containers, such as small glass canning jars.

1. In a food processor, add the arugula, mint, and garlic. Pulse to combine.
2. Add the cashews and Parmesan and pulse to combine. While pulsing, carefully stream olive oil into the processor until the mixture comes together.
3. Add the salt and lemon juice and stir to combine.

Storage Tip When storing pesto in the refrigerator, top off the jar with a little olive oil before sealing.

Storage Instructions Transfer to an airtight container and store in the refrigerator for up to 4 days.

Pumpkin Seed Pesto

YIELDS ½ CUP

PREP TIME: 5 MIN

FLAVOR NOTE:
NUTTY

**VEGETARIAN, 30 MIN OR LESS,
GLUTEN FREE, NUT FREE**

1 cup loosely packed fresh basil

2 cloves garlic, peeled

¼ cup pumpkin seeds

½ cup grated Parmesan

¼ teaspoon kosher salt

⅓ cup extra-virgin olive oil

Special Equipment: Food Processor

Pesto can be made with a variety of different nuts and/or seeds. Pumpkin seeds, also known as pepitas, are the star of this pesto. Don't let the green color alarm you—they're supposed to be that way. Combined with traditional basil, they offer a fresh twist on the classic Genovese pesto.

1 In a food processor, add the basil and garlic. Pulse to combine.
2 Add the pumpkin seeds, Parmesan, and salt. Pulse to combine. While pulsing, carefully stream the olive oil into the food processor until the mixture is combined.

Storage Tip When storing pesto in the refrigerator, top off the jar with a little olive oil before sealing.
Storage Instructions Transfer to an airtight container and store in the refrigerator for up to 4 days.

Lemon, Artichoke, and Pine Nut Pesto

YIELDS ½ CUP

PREP TIME: 10 MIN

FLAVOR NOTES:
NUTTY, SAVORY

VEGETARIAN, 30 MIN OR LESS, GLUTEN FREE

1 cup artichoke hearts, drained

2 cloves garlic, peeled

¼ cup pine nuts

½ cup grated Parmesan

¼ teaspoon kosher salt

½ teaspoon lemon juice

⅓ cup extra-virgin olive oil

Special Equipment: Food Processor

For a fast and flavorful pesto, this Lemon, Artichoke and Pine Nut Pesto recipe is a go-to. It will add texture and depth to any dish, and it's also versatile enough to be used as a condiment. Here's a tip: Toast the pine nuts prior to adding them to the food processor for even more flavor and texture. It's a quick and easy step that yields big results. If you prefer, you can also substitute walnuts for pine nuts.

1 In a food processor, add the artichoke hearts and garlic and pulse to combine. Add the pine nuts, Parmesan, and salt. Pulse to combine.

2 Add the lemon juice. While pulsing, carefully stream olive oil into the food processor until the mixture comes together.

Storage Tip When storing pesto in the refrigerator, top off the jar with a little olive oil before sealing.

Storage Instructions Transfer to an airtight container and store in the refrigerator for up to 4 days.

Kale and Pistachio Pesto

YIELDS ½ CUP

PREP TIME: 10 MIN

FLAVOR NOTE:
NUTTY

**VEGETARIAN, 30 MIN OR LESS,
GLUTEN FREE, 5-INGREDIENT**

1 cup chopped kale

2 cloves garlic, peeled

⅓ cup shelled pistachios

½ cup grated Parmesan

¼ teaspoon fresh lemon juice

⅓ cup extra-virgin olive oil

Special Equipment: Food Processor

I adore pistachios, and I'm not sure why they're not used more frequently in pestos. This combination is magical, and if I had to pick one pesto, it would be this one. The hardest part will be shelling the pistachios. If you'd like to save your manicure and time, you can buy pistachios pre-shelled. Again, toasting the nuts prior to using them is optional but encouraged to bring out that extra flavor.

1   In a food processor, add the kale and garlic and pulse to combine. Add the pistachios and Parmesan and pulse again.

2   Add the lemon juice. While pulsing, carefully stream the olive oil into the food processor until the mixture comes together.

Storage Tip When storing pesto in the refrigerator, top off the jar with a little olive oil before sealing.

Storage Instructions Transfer to an airtight container and store in the refrigerator for up to 4 days.

Spinach and Truffle Oil Pesto

YIELDS ½ CUP

PREP TIME: 10 MIN

FLAVOR NOTE:
NUTTY

**VEGETARIAN, 30 MIN OR LESS,
GLUTEN FREE, 5-INGREDIENT**

1 cup packed fresh spinach

3 cloves garlic, peeled

⅓ cup pine nuts

⅓ cup grated Parmesan

¼ teaspoon kosher salt

¼ cup extra-virgin olive oil

¼ teaspoon truffle oil

Special Equipment: Food Processor

Truffle oil is a modern way to infuse truffle flavor into dishes, including pesto. I prefer to use it sparingly because it's incredibly potent and can easily go from "Oh, my gosh this is amazing!" to very overpowering. It is the perfect finishing touch to this spinach and pine nut pesto. Toss with your favorite short pasta for something out of the ordinary. If you prefer a looser pesto, simply add additional olive oil until it's your desired consistency.

1 In a food processor, add the spinach and garlic and pulse to combine. Add the pine nuts, Parmesan, and salt. Pulse to combine.

2 While pulsing, carefully stream the olive and truffle oils into the food processor until the mixture is combined.

Storage Tip When storing pesto in the refrigerator, top off the jar with a little olive oil before sealing.
Storage Instructions Transfer to an airtight container and store in the refrigerator for up to 4 days.

Preserved Lemon and Cashew Pesto

YIELDS ½ CUP

PREP TIME: 10 MIN

FLAVOR NOTES:
NUTTY, ZESTY

**VEGETARIAN, 30 MIN OR LESS,
GLUTEN FREE, 5-INGREDIENT**

½ tablespoon preserved lemon peel

4 large basil leaves

1 clove garlic, peeled

¼ cup cashews

½ cup grated Parmesan

⅓ cup extra-virgin olive oil

⅛ teaspoon freshly ground
  black pepper

Special Equipment: Food Processor

Preserved lemons are typically found in Moroccan and Middle Eastern cuisine but are making their way into the mainstream these days. They add that lovely, intense lemon flavor without the typical sourness. You can preserve your own lemons at home, but if that's not an option, you can look for preserved lemons in the international aisle at your grocery store or find them for sale online. Preserved lemon mixed with basil, cashews, and a sprinkling of freshly ground black pepper is a flavor explosion of the best kind.

1 In a food processor, add the preserved lemon peel, basil, and garlic and pulse to combine. Add the cashews and Parmesan. Pulse to combine.

2 While pulsing, carefully stream olive oil into the food processor until the mixture is combined. Season with pepper and stir to combine.

Storage Tip When storing pesto in the refrigerator, top off the jar with a little olive oil before sealing.

Storage Instructions Transfer to an airtight container and store in the refrigerator for up to 4 days.

Sun-Dried Tomato Pesto with Walnuts and Black Pepper

YIELDS ½ CUP

PREP TIME: 10 MIN

FLAVOR NOTES:
NUTTY, PEPPERY

VEGETARIAN, 30 MIN OR LESS, GLUTEN FREE, 5-INGREDIENT

2 tablespoons chopped sun-dried tomatoes (oil-packed), ¼ cup oil retained

1 cup packed spinach

3 cloves garlic, peeled

¼ cup walnuts

⅓ cup grated Parmesan

2 tablespoons extra-virgin olive oil

⅛ teaspoon freshly ground black pepper

Special Equipment: Food Processor

Sun-dried tomatoes in olive oil pack a powerful flavor punch. As the name implies, these tomatoes are dried under the sun, concentrating their flavor and preserving them before they are packed in olive oil. In this recipe, we've meshed sun-dried tomatoes with walnuts and a combination of the infused oil with regular olive oil. Finish with a grinding of freshly ground black pepper for a fantastic versatile pesto.

1 In a food processor, add the sun-dried tomatoes, spinach, and garlic and pulse to combine. Add the walnuts and Parmesan. Pulse to combine.

2 While pulsing, carefully stream the olive oil and oil from the tomatoes into the food processor, mixing until everything is combined. Season with pepper and stir to combine.

Option Tip Don't discard the olive oil the sun-dried tomatoes are packed in. Instead, use it to infuse even more tomato flavor into your recipes.
Storage Instructions Transfer to an airtight container and store in the refrigerator for up to 4 days.

Grilled Spring Onion Pesto

YIELDS ½ CUP

PREP TIME: 10 MIN
COOK TIME: 5 MIN

FLAVOR NOTES:
NUTTY, SAVORY

**VEGETARIAN, 30 MIN OR LESS,
GLUTEN FREE, 5-INGREDIENT**

1 spring onion, white end trimmed

1 cup chopped kale

2 cloves garlic, peeled

¼ cup cashews

¼ cup grated Parmesan

½ cup extra-virgin olive oil

Freshly ground black pepper

Special Equipment: Food Processor

Whether you call them scallions, spring onions, or green onions, they are all the same thing. Green onions have a milder flavor than a traditional onion, making them a great option for pesto. Once the ends are trimmed, they can be eaten raw or cooked. I've taken the cooked route and grilled them here. It takes just a minute or so for them to wilt to perfection, then they're mixed with kale and cashews for a refreshingly unusual pesto. Just don't forget the breath mints after enjoying this one!

1 Heat a grill pan over medium heat. Add the onion and grill until softened, turning as necessary.

2 In a food processor, add the onion, kale, and garlic. Pulse to combine. Add the cashews and Parmesan and pulse to combine. While pulsing, carefully stream the olive oil into the food processor until the mixture comes together. Season with pepper and mix to combine.

Ingredient Tip Toast the nuts prior to making the pesto for an extra burst of flavor.

Storage Instructions Transfer to an airtight container and store in the refrigerator for up to 4 days.

Basil, Garlic, and Chile Pesto

YIELDS ½ CUP

PREP TIME: 10 MIN

FLAVOR NOTES:
NUTTY, SPICY

**VEGETARIAN, 30 MIN OR LESS,
GLUTEN FREE, 5-INGREDIENT**

1 cup packed fresh basil

2 cloves garlic, peeled

¼ cup cashews

1 small red chile pepper,
  seeds removed

¼ cup grated Parmesan

½ cup extra-virgin olive oil

Special Equipment: Food Processor

This pesto is not for the faint of heart. If you like your pesto with a kick, you're in the right place. We're using red chile peppers to bring the heat factor. They are long and thin, typically 2 or 3 inches in length. It's always a great idea to wear gloves when handling and cooking with peppers. On the other hand, you could also substitute ½ teaspoon red pepper flakes for a less spicy pesto.

1   In a food processor, add the basil and garlic. Pulse to combine. Add the cashews, chile pepper, and Parmesan and pulse to combine.

2   While pulsing, carefully stream the olive oil into the food processor until the mixture comes together.

Ingredient Tip Leaving the seeds in the hot pepper will add additional heat to the dish.

Storage Instructions Transfer to an airtight container and store in the refrigerator for up to 4 days.

CHAPTER 6

MEAT

IF YOU ARE LOOKING FOR A STICK-TO-YOUR-ribs kind of sauce, then you have landed in the right place. Meat-based sauces are exactly that—they're a carnivore's dream: thick, rich, and hearty.

The most famous Italian meat sauce has got to be Bolognese, so named because it hails from Bologna, Italy. It develops its deep flavors over hours of slow, gentle simmering. Up until now, it has been what I like to call a Sunday sauce because of the time requirements. I've put a modern twist on this classic meat sauce by taking it off the stovetop and putting it into the pressure cooker instead, saving hours of time without sacrificing any flavor.

In this chapter, you will find recipes that incorporate a wide variety of meats, including beef, pork, turkey, veal, and lamb, as well as a variety of different cuts of meat (ground, shank, short rib, etc.).

I've included five ragùs—thick, chunky, meaty sauces—to tempt your taste buds and challenge your idea of a meat sauce: Country Ham Ragù (page 74), Lamb Shank Ragù with Red Wine and Dates (page 75), Pork Ragù with Toasted Bread Crumbs (page 76), Sausage and Fennel Ragù with Roasted Red Peppers (page 79), and finally, a Turkey-Prosciutto Ragù with Nutmeg and Sage (page 81). Don't they sound delicious?

Another classic we couldn't leave out of this chapter is the Roman dish carbonara. It is hands down my favorite pasta dish of all time. Traditionally, it's made using *guanciale* or pancetta. Our modern twist adds squash, which gives it an even silkier, creamier feel. We recommend garnishing the dish with fried sage leaves, not only for presentation, but because they complement the pasta and the squash famously well.

Braising is one of my favorite methods of cooking meats. Braising is simply searing the meat first and then cooking it slowly in a liquid in a closed container (I use an oven-safe Dutch oven with lid). This process produces fall-off-the-bone-tender meat every time.

There are three recipes in this chapter that are braised: Short Ribs with Bourbon Reduction (page 78), Lamb Shank Ragù with Red Wine and Dates (page 75), and Veal Sauce with Grilled Lemon (page 77). They are all insanely delicious and worth the time they take. I hope you'll add them to your weekend menu-planning. If you're entertaining, these are great menu ideas because the majority of the magic happens in the oven, freeing you up to do all of the other host/hostess duties.

No matter your meat preference, I hope you'll find a recipe in this chapter that piques your interest and gets you into the kitchen to cook. Don't be afraid to step outside of your comfort zone and try something that perhaps you've not tried before. Who knows? You may find a new favorite.

Squash Carbonara with Pancetta

SERVES 4

PREP TIME: 5 MIN
COOK TIME: 15 MIN

FLAVOR NOTES:
SAVORY, RICH

**NUT FREE, 30 MIN OR LESS,
GLUTEN FREE**

2 tablespoons extra-virgin olive oil

4 slices pancetta, chopped

3 cloves garlic, minced

2 whole eggs plus 1 additional
   egg yolk, beaten

1 cup grated Parmesan

½ cup grated pecorino cheese

¼ to ½ teaspoon freshly
   ground black pepper

1 cup butternut squash purée

Spaghetti alla Carbonara is my all-time favorite pasta dish. To me, it's the epitome of comfort food. The beauty of carbonara is in simplicity and in its preparation. Timing is key: The spaghetti needs to be hot when added to the sauce, so that the heat from the pasta cooks the eggs. The twist for this carbonara is the butternut squash purée. It adds an additional layer of flavor and creaminess, and the crunch comes from the crispy pancetta bits.

1 Heat the olive oil over medium heat in a 5-quart Dutch oven. Add the pancetta and cook until crispy. Using a slotted spoon, carefully transfer pancetta to a plate lined with paper towels. Set aside.

2 In the same Dutch oven, add the garlic and sauté until fragrant, being careful not to let it burn.

3 In a small bowl, whisk together the eggs and cheeses. Season with black pepper.

4 Transfer cooked pasta directly into the pan with the oil and garlic. Toss until coated. Remove from the heat. Add the egg mixture and toss until completely coated.

5 Add the squash purée and toss to coat. Use reserved pasta water to thin the sauce, if necessary.

6 Garnish with crispy pancetta and additional black pepper.

Option Tip Garnish with fried sage leaves.
Storage Instructions Transfer to an airtight container and store in the refrigerator for up to 4 days.

Pressure Cooker Bolognese

SERVES 6

PREP TIME: 15 MIN
COOK TIME: 30 MIN, PLUS TIME FOR MACHINE TO COME TO PRESSURE

FLAVOR NOTES:
SAVORY, RICH

NUT FREE, DAIRY FREE

2 tablespoons extra-virgin olive oil

2 carrots, peeled and minced

2 stalks celery, ends trimmed, minced

1 clove garlic, minced

1 small onion, minced

1 pound ground beef

1 pound ground veal

1 teaspoon kosher salt

¼ teaspoon freshly ground black pepper

1 (6-ounce) can tomato paste

½ bottle red wine

Special Equipment: Electric Pressure Cooker

Bolognese is a meat-based sauce that hails from Bologna, Italy. It is the epitome of a Sunday sauce, due to its long, slow simmering requirements. I've taken a modern twist on this classic sauce by preparing it in a pressure cooker, saving loads of time and making it perfect for any night of the week.

1   Set the pressure cooker to Sauté. Add the olive oil. When the oil is hot, add the carrots, celery, garlic, and onion. Sauté until softened, stirring as necessary.

2   Add the ground beef and veal and season with salt and pepper. Cook until the meat has browned. Drain and discard grease.

3   Add the tomato paste and wine. Stir to combine.

4   Secure the lid and set the valve to the sealing position. Choose the Manual program and set a timer for 20 minutes. When the time is complete, carefully do a quick release (according to the manufacturer's directions).

Ingredient Tip Pair with tagliatelle or pappardelle, or use this sauce to make Lasagna alla Bolognese or as part of stuffed shells.
Storage Instructions Transfer to an airtight container and store in the refrigerator for up to 4 days.

Country Ham Ragù

SERVES 4

PREP TIME: 5 MIN
COOK TIME: 25 MIN

FLAVOR NOTES:
SAVORY, RICH

NUT FREE, DAIRY FREE, 30 MIN OR LESS

1 tablespoon extra-virgin olive oil

½ onion, minced

2 slices country ham, diced

1 tablespoon tomato paste

¼ teaspoon allspice

1 cup dry white wine

½ cup chicken stock

Country ham is a variety of ham that is preserved by curing and smoking. It's heavily salted, so we don't add any additional salt during cooking. The allspice is a great sweet balance to the salty nature of the ham. It's all brought together with tomato paste, wine, and stock. If you have homemade stock, even better. Serve with spaghetti or it would also be amazing over polenta or gnocchi.

1 In a 3.5-quart Dutch oven, heat the olive oil over medium heat. Add the onion and sauté until softened.

2 Add the country ham and cook until browned. Add the tomato paste and allspice and stir to combine.

3 Add the wine and allow the sauce to simmer until it has reduced by half. Add the chicken stock and simmer until warmed through.

Ingredient Tip If you're using store-bought chicken stock, go with a low-sodium option. This sauce would also work great over zucchini noodles.
Storage Instructions Transfer to an airtight container and store in the refrigerator for up to 4 days.

Lamb Shank Ragù with Red Wine and Dates

SERVES 4 TO 6

PREP TIME: 15 MIN
COOK TIME: 2 HRS

FLAVOR NOTES:
SAVORY, RICH

NUT FREE, DAIRY FREE, GLUTEN FREE

2 pounds lamb shanks

½ teaspoon kosher salt

¼ teaspoon freshly ground black pepper

2 tablespoons extra-virgin olive oil

2 carrots, peeled and minced

2 stalks celery, ends trimmed, minced

2 cloves garlic, minced

½ cup red wine

14½ ounces diced tomatoes

1 cup chicken stock

2 Medjool dates, pitted and chopped

2 or 3 sprigs fresh thyme

Braising meat is a beautiful way to easily achieve fall-off-the-bone-tender meat. Be sure to use an oven-safe Dutch oven, as this dish will be going from the stovetop directly into the oven for braising. Take care to brown the shanks well on all sides before moving on to the next step. This is the step where we develop those wonderful layers of flavors.

1 Preheat the oven to 350°F.

2 Season the lamb shanks on both sides with salt and pepper. Heat the olive oil in an oven-safe 5-quart Dutch oven over medium heat. Add the lamb and brown on all sides. Transfer the seared lamb to a plate and set aside.

3 Add the carrots, celery, and garlic to the Dutch oven. Cook until softened.

4 Add the wine, tomatoes, chicken stock, dates, and thyme. Season with additional salt and pepper, as necessary. Stir to combine. Return the lamb to the pot and cover with a lid.

5 Carefully transfer the pot to the oven and allow to braise for about 1½ hours, or until the meat is falling-off-the-bone tender.

6 Shred the meat and discard the bones. Return the shredded meat to the sauce.

Ingredient Tip Pair this sauce with pappardelle.
Storage Instructions Transfer to an airtight container and store in the refrigerator for up to 4 days.

Pork Ragù with Toasted Bread Crumbs

SERVES 4 TO 6

PREP TIME: 15 MIN
COOK TIME: 45 MIN

FLAVOR NOTES:
SAVORY, RICH

NUT FREE, DAIRY FREE

3 tablespoons extra-virgin olive oil

2 carrots, peeled and minced

1 leek, white and light green portions only, thinly sliced

2 stalks celery, trimmed, minced

2 cloves garlic, minced

1½ pounds ground pork

1 (8-ounce) can tomato sauce

1 cup chicken stock

1 teaspoon kosher salt

¼ teaspoon freshly ground black pepper

2 tablespoons sun-dried tomato spread

½ cup panko bread crumbs

Ragù is the term used to describe a chunky, meat-based sauce in Italian cuisine. It can come with any type of meat; this ragù is pork-based. We're starting with a twist on the traditional soffrito, *by swapping out the onion in favor of milder leek. Once the ground pork is cooked and the next ingredients are added to the party pot, it simmers long enough for the flavors to mingle and develop.*

1   Heat the olive oil in a 5-quart Dutch oven over medium heat. Add the carrots, leek, celery, and garlic. Sauté until softened.

2   Add the ground pork and cook until browned, stirring as necessary.

3   Add the tomato sauce, stock, salt, pepper, and sun-dried tomato spread. Stir to combine. Reduce to a simmer and cook for 30 minutes.

4   In a separate, dry skillet, toast the bread crumbs over medium heat until browned, stirring constantly so they don't burn.

5   Once the pasta is plated, top each serving with sauce and toasted bread crumbs.

Storage Tip If you're planning on keeping this for leftovers, keep the bread crumbs separate from the pasta so they do not become soggy in the refrigerator.

Storage Instructions Transfer to an airtight container and store in the refrigerator for up to 4 days.

Veal Sauce with Grilled Lemon

SERVES 2 TO 4

PREP TIME: 15 MIN
COOK TIME: 1 HR 15 MIN

FLAVOR NOTES:
SAVORY, RICH

NUT FREE

2 large thick bone-in veal chops

½ teaspoon kosher salt

¼ teaspoon freshly ground
  black pepper

2 tablespoons extra-virgin olive oil

½ onion, minced

2 cloves garlic, minced

1 cup dry white wine

1 tablespoon unsalted butter

1½ cups chicken stock

1 lemon, halved

Browned and braised is the name of the game. Large, thick, bone-in chops are browned until golden. Onions and garlic are sautéed until fragrant and then the pan is deglazed with white wine, allowing you to scrape up all the flavor that is hanging on to the pan. Chicken stock is added, and then it's into the oven to cook until the sauce thickens and the meat is tender. Serve with egg noodles for a complete meal.

1   Preheat the oven to 350°F.

2   Season the veal chops on both sides with salt and pepper. Heat the olive oil in an oven-safe 5-quart Dutch oven over medium heat. Add the veal and brown on both sides. Transfer the veal to a plate and set aside.

3   Add the onion and garlic and sauté until softened, being careful not to burn the garlic.

4   Add the wine and carefully deglaze the pan, scraping the bottom to release all the browned bits. Season with additional salt and pepper. Add the butter and chicken stock. Return the veal to the Dutch oven and cover with a lid.

5   Carefully transfer the whole pot to the oven and cook for about 1 hour, or until the meat is falling-off-the-bone tender.

6   Place the lemon onto a hot grill pan and grill until marks appear. Squeeze the lemon over the veal chops and serve.

Substitution Tip If you can't find veal chops, you can substitute veal shanks here instead.
Storage Instructions Transfer to an airtight container and store in the refrigerator for up to 4 days.

Short Ribs with Bourbon Reduction

SERVES 4

PREP TIME: 15 MIN
COOK TIME: 3 HRS 15 MIN

FLAVOR NOTES:
SAVORY, RICH

NUT FREE, DAIRY FREE, ONE POT

2½ pounds bone-in beef short ribs

½ teaspoon kosher salt

¼ teaspoon freshly ground
 black pepper

2 tablespoons chopped fresh thyme

2 tablespoons chopped fresh sage

2 tablespoons extra-virgin olive oil

2 carrots, peeled and minced

2 stalks celery, ends trimmed, minced

1 leek, dark green ends
 discarded, thinly sliced

1 teaspoon garlic paste

½ cup bourbon

2½ cups chicken stock

If I had to tell you just one thing about this recipe, it would be that these beef short ribs are worth the effort and the wait. The majority of the time involved is spent letting the ribs braise in the oven. Braised short ribs are typically braised with wine and stock and—while that method is delicious—substituting bourbon for the wine is a game-changer. I'm incredibly smitten with this recipe, and I think you will be, too.

1 Preheat the oven to 350°F.

2 Season the short ribs with salt, pepper, thyme, and sage. Set aside.

3 Heat the olive oil in an oven-safe 5-quart Dutch oven over medium heat. Sear the short ribs on all sides until they are nicely browned. Set the seared ribs aside.

4 In the same Dutch oven, add the carrots, celery, leek, and garlic paste. Sauté until the vegetables have softened.

5 Add the bourbon to deglaze the pan, scraping the browned bits from the bottom of the Dutch oven.

6 Add the stock and return the short ribs to the pan, cover with a lid, and carefully transfer to the oven. Bake covered for 2 hours. Uncover and continue cooking an additional 30 minutes to 1 hour, until the meat is tender and shreds when pierced with a fork.

Ingredient Tip You can substitute 2 cloves minced garlic for garlic paste.
Storage Instructions Transfer to an airtight container and store in the refrigerator for up to 4 days.

Sausage and Fennel Ragù with Roasted Red Peppers

SERVES 4 TO 6

PREP TIME: 10 MIN
COOK TIME: 45 MIN

FLAVOR NOTES:
SAVORY, RICH

NUT FREE, DAIRY FREE, ONE POT

2 tablespoons extra-virgin olive oil

½ onion, minced

1 teaspoon garlic paste

1 pound mild ground Italian sausage

½ cup dry white wine

14½ ounces diced tomatoes

1 (15-ounce) can tomato sauce

7 ounces roasted red
  peppers, chopped

½ teaspoon fennel seeds

½ teaspoon kosher salt

¼ teaspoon freshly ground
  black pepper

Simple, convenient, and delicious—perfect for a weeknight meal. Sausage and fennel are a pair made for each other. With a quick sauté of onion and sausage, the rest of the ingredients go into the Dutch oven to simmer to thick and bubbly perfection. Add a short pasta such as rigatoni to the pan for a complete meal. If you're looking for a little kick, you can add ½ teaspoon of red pepper flakes to the mix while cooking.

1 Heat the olive oil in a 3.5- or 5-quart Dutch oven over medium heat. Add the onion and garlic and sauté until softened. Add the sausage and cook until browned, stirring as necessary.

2 Add the wine and simmer until the liquid has reduced by half. Add the tomatoes, tomato sauce, and roasted red peppers. Stir to combine and season with the fennel seeds, salt, and pepper.

3 Reduce the heat to a simmer and cook for 30 minutes, stirring occasionally.

Substitution Tip If you can't find ground Italian sausage, you can purchase links and simply remove and discard the casing.

Storage Instructions Transfer to an airtight container and store in the refrigerator for up to 4 days.

Amatriciana

SERVES 4 TO 6

PREP TIME: 5 MIN
COOK TIME: 30 MIN

FLAVOR NOTES:
SAVORY, RICH

NUT FREE, ONE POT

4 slices pancetta, chopped

1 small onion, minced

28 ounces crushed tomatoes

¼ teaspoon red pepper flakes

¼ teaspoon kosher salt

¼ cup pecorino cheese

A traditional amatriciana is made using guanciale *(dried pork cheek).* Guanciale *isn't always widely available, so I opt for pancetta in this version. This is a simple and flavorful weeknight sauce. You can use fresh tomatoes or crushed canned tomatoes, depending on the season. Pair the sauce with bucatini, the long, thick spaghetti-esque noodle that has a hole through the middle.*

1 Place the pancetta into a 3.5-quart Dutch oven and cook over medium heat until crispy. Once browned, carefully remove the pancetta with a slotted spoon and transfer to a plate lined with paper towels.

2 In the same Dutch oven, add the onion and sauté until softened, stirring as necessary.

3 Add the tomatoes, red pepper flakes, and salt. Stir to combine and allow to simmer for 15 minutes.

4 Add the cheese and stir to combine. Garnish with the crispy pancetta.

Ingredient Tip Check if your local butcher carries *guanciale*. If you can find it, the added richness is worth the extra trouble.
Storage Instructions Transfer to an airtight container and store in the refrigerator for up to 4 days.

Turkey-Prosciutto Ragù with Nutmeg and Sage

SERVES 4 TO 6

PREP TIME: 15 MIN
COOK TIME: 45 MIN

FLAVOR NOTES:
SAVORY, RICH

NUT FREE, ONE POT

2 tablespoons extra-virgin olive oil

2 slices prosciutto, roughly torn

2 carrots, peeled and minced

2 stalks celery, ends trimmed, minced

½ onion, minced

2 cloves garlic, minced

1 pound ground turkey

1 teaspoon fresh sage

1 teaspoon nutmeg

1½ teaspoons kosher salt

1 cup dry white wine

½ cup chicken stock

28 ounces crushed tomatoes

3 tablespoons tomato paste

This turkey ragù is brimming with the flavors of sage and nutmeg. Turkey absorbs flavors beautifully and is available in most grocery stores nationwide. This is a sauce that's ready in about an hour, and most of that is simmer time. Here's a great sauce (and soup) tip: If you happen to have a Parmesan rind around, add it to the sauce while it's simmering for even more depth. I like to save my rinds for just these occasions.

1   Heat the olive oil in a 5-quart Dutch oven over medium heat. Add the prosciutto and cook until crispy. Carefully transfer the prosciutto to a plate lined with paper towels and set aside.

2   Add the carrots, celery, onion, and garlic to the Dutch oven and sauté until softened. Add the ground turkey, sage, nutmeg, and salt. Cook until browned, stirring as necessary.

3   Add the wine and allow the liquid to reduce by half. Add the stock, tomatoes, and tomato paste. Stir well to combine. Reduce the heat and simmer for 30 minutes.

4   Once plated, garnish each plate of pasta with the crispy prosciutto.

Ingredient Tip Pair this sauce with a thin pasta, like spaghetti.
Storage Instructions Transfer to an airtight container and store in the refrigerator for up to 4 days.

CHAPTER 7

VEGAN

ALTHOUGH THERE ARE MANY VEGETARIAN recipes in this book, I'm including a chapter that is specifically vegan-friendly. If you've fallen on this chapter, you probably are already familiar with veganism, but for those who are not—or are vegan-curious—it means the recipes in this chapter exclude meat, eggs, dairy products, and any other animal-derived ingredients.

I don't believe you have to be a vegan to enjoy these recipes. I am not vegan myself, but I do occasionally enjoy a variety of plant-based recipes. The Hearty Lentil and Mushroom Bolognese (page 86) in this chapter is one of my favorite recipes. It's hearty, "meaty," and completely satisfying. It uses small green lentils, which hold up well during longer cooking periods and maintain a nice bite to help give the dish that stick-to-your-ribs feeling. Curling up with a big bowl of it over the fall and winter seasons is something I always look forward to. It would be perfect to eat alone as a stew, over pasta, or even over zoodles. Options: we love them!

A "cheese" sauce for just about any occasion— including eating with a spoon if that's your style—can be found in the "Cheesy" Cashew Cream Sauce (page 90). It's a quick and easy recipe, made entirely in a blender. That's right, no cooking involved. Cashews are found in many vegan recipes for good reason: they're buttery, creamy, and versatile. Use this "cheese" sauce with any of your favorite pasta types. If you find the sauce to be a little too thick (a strong blender will do that), simply add a little more vegetable broth and mix until it's at your desired consistency.

My twist on ratatouille—Eggplant, Roasted Red Pepper, and Tomato Sauce (page 93)—is another good option. Besides being delicious, eggplant is a great "meat" alternative. For this recipe, we've roasted the eggplant until it's completely tender. This step can be done well in advance, perhaps when you already have the oven on for another recipe. The eggplant skin is easily removed, leaving the soft interior to add to the sauce. After it's simmered and the flavors have mingled, you can eat the sauce as is or use an immersion blender to make it silky smooth.

I've adapted another classic in this chapter, Vegan Vodka Sauce (page 88). This vegan version uses coconut milk instead of cream and yields a hefty portion, making it perfect to cook once, use twice. Leftovers are a good thing in my book.

Pesto is another versatile sauce and condiment that can even be used as a spread. While there is an entire chapter devoted to pesto in this book, I couldn't resist including one more: bright, beautiful, Pea Pesto Garnished with Microgreens (page 91). You'll be surprised how many ways you'll end up enjoying this recipe.

I hope you find something new to try in this chapter. 🍎

Hearty Lentil and Mushroom Bolognese

SERVES 6

PREP TIME: 15 MIN
COOK TIME: 1 HR

FLAVOR NOTES:
SAVORY, RICH

NUT FREE, ONE POT, VEGAN

2 tablespoons extra-virgin olive oil

2 carrots, peeled and minced

2 stalks celery, ends trimmed, minced

½ onion, minced

2 cloves garlic, minced

8 ounces baby bella
  mushrooms, chopped

1 cup dry red wine

4 tablespoons tomato paste

2 cups vegetable stock

14½ ounces crushed tomatoes

1 cup small green lentils

1 teaspoon kosher salt

¼ teaspoon freshly ground
  black pepper

½ teaspoon Mediterranean oregano

3 bay leaves

This is a great vegan alternative to the classic Bolognese. It's hearty, rich, delicious, and made in just one pot. Lentils are a great form of protein and fiber. We've chosen small green lentils for this recipe. They have a stronger earthy flavor than other lentils, and they hold their firmness during longer cooking times, making them perfect for this recipe.

1 Heat the olive oil in a 5-quart Dutch oven over medium heat. Add the carrots, celery, onion, and garlic and sauté until softened.

2 Add the mushrooms and cook until they've released their water, stirring as necessary.

3 Add the wine and simmer until the liquid has reduced by half. Stir in the tomato paste, stock, tomatoes, and lentils. Season with salt, pepper, and oregano.

4 Bring the sauce to a boil. Once boiling, add the bay leaves and reduce the heat, allowing the sauce to simmer for 45 minutes. Remove and discard the bay leaves prior to serving.

Option Tip Whole vegetables cost less, but if you'd like to save time, you can purchase presliced mushrooms and other vegetables.

Ingredient Tip Using tomato paste in a tube is much more convenient for measuring, and you can save any leftover paste to use later (unless you plan on using an entire can's worth).

Storage Instructions Transfer to an airtight container and store in the refrigerator for up to 4 days.

Pumpkin Sauce with Crispy Mushrooms

SERVES 4

PREP TIME: 10 MIN
COOK TIME: 20 MIN

FLAVOR NOTES:
SAVORY, RICH

**NUT FREE, ONE POT, VEGAN,
30 MIN OR LESS**

3 tablespoons extra-virgin
olive oil, divided

1 tablespoon plant-based butter

8 ounces baby bella
mushrooms, sliced

½ teaspoon kosher salt

¼ teaspoon freshly ground
black pepper

¼ cup minced red onion

1 cup dry white wine

½ cup pumpkin purée

2 fresh sage leaves, minced

1 cup reserved pasta water
or vegetable stock

Pumpkin isn't just for desserts—it's quite delicious in savory dishes like this sauce. The trick to getting crispy mushrooms is to give them room in the pan and leave them in a single layer, allowing them to brown and turn crispy. This creates a wonderful texture which complements the pumpkin.

1   Heat 2 tablespoons of oil and the plant-based butter in a heavy-bottomed saucepan over medium heat. Add the mushrooms, season with salt and pepper, and cook until they have released their water and browned. Transfer the mushrooms to a plate lined with paper towels and set aside.

2   Add the remaining oil to the saucepan and heat over medium heat. Add the onion, cooking until softened. Add the wine and simmer until the liquid has reduced by half.

3   Add the pumpkin purée and season with additional salt and pepper, as needed. Add the sage and stir to combine. Cook the sauce until just warmed through. If the consistency is too thick, add reserved pasta water or vegetable stock to thin it out a bit.

4   Toss with pasta and top with crispy mushrooms.

Ingredient Tip Be sure to choose a can of pumpkin purée at the store and **not** pumpkin pie filling to avoid the added sugar and spices in pie fillings. It's a common mistake! The fall is a great time to stock up on cans of purée while they are on sale.

Storage Instructions Transfer to an airtight container and store in the refrigerator for up to 4 days.

Vegan Vodka Sauce

SERVES 6

PREP TIME: 10 MIN
COOK TIME: 45 MIN

FLAVOR NOTES:
SAVORY, RICH

NUT FREE, ONE POT, VEGAN

4 tablespoons extra-virgin olive oil

1 small onion, minced

2 or 3 cloves garlic, minced

32 ounces crushed tomatoes

1 cup vegetable stock

1 teaspoon kosher salt

½ teaspoon freshly ground
  black pepper

1 cup vodka

1½ cups coconut milk, stirred

2 or 3 basil leaves, sliced
  thinly, for garnish

Vodka sauce is beloved by many, and you can frequently find it on restaurant menus everywhere. Vodka sauce is typically paired with penne, though I also like it paired with spaghetti. The sauce is creamy, silky, and comforting, and it also happens to be incredibly easy to make at home. The traditional vodka sauce involves a base of tomatoes, vodka, and cream. In this vegan version, we substitute coconut milk for the cream.

1 Heat the olive oil in a heavy-bottomed saucepan over medium heat. Add the onion and garlic and sauté until softened, stirring as necessary to avoid burning the garlic.

2 Add the tomatoes and stock and season with salt and pepper. Stir to combine. Reduce the heat to low and simmer for 15 minutes.

3 Add the vodka and coconut milk and stir to combine. Taste for seasoning, adding additional salt and pepper, if necessary. Continue simmering for an additional 15 minutes.

4 Toss cooked pasta with the sauce and garnish with basil.

Helpful Tip Thin your sauce with reserved pasta water, if necessary, to achieve your desired consistency.

Storage Instructions Transfer to an airtight container and store in the refrigerator for up to 4 days.

Roasted Sweet Potato and Tomato Sauce

YIELDS 4 CUPS

PREP TIME: 5 MIN
COOK TIME: 15 MIN

FLAVOR NOTES:
SAVORY, RICH

NUT FREE, VEGAN, 30 MIN OR LESS

1 large sweet potato,
  peeled and cubed

14½ ounces diced tomatoes

½ cup reserved sweet potato water,
  from boiling the potatoes

¼ cup coconut milk, stirred

2 tablespoons extra-virgin olive oil

½ teaspoon kosher salt

¼ teaspoon freshly ground
  black pepper

2 basil leaves, thinly sliced, for garnish

Special Equipment: Blender

Sweet potatoes are incredibly versatile. They can be baked, boiled, fried, smashed, and mashed. They can handle the heat. While at first thought, sweet potatoes and tomatoes would seem like an odd combination, they work incredibly well together. The odd couple, if you will. If you have a little extra time and want to roast the sweet potato first, that would make a delicious swap instead of boiling, which happens to be the only cooking in the recipe.

1 Place the cubed sweet potato into a pot and cover with water. Bring to a boil and cook until potatoes are fork-tender.

2 Transfer the cooked sweet potatoes to the blender. Add the tomatoes, reserved sweet potato water, coconut milk, olive oil, salt, and pepper. Blend until smooth.

3 If the sauce is too thick, thin with additional reserved sweet potato water.

4 Once the sauce is tossed with pasta, garnish with basil.

Time-Saving Tip The sweet potatoes can be prepared in advance to save time.

Storage Instructions Transfer to an airtight container and store in the refrigerator for up to 4 days.

"Cheesy" Cashew Cream Sauce

YIELDS 3 CUPS

PREP TIME: 5 MIN

FLAVOR NOTES:
SAVORY, RICH

**VEGAN, 30 MIN OR LESS,
5-INGREDIENT**

1 cup cashews

2 tablespoons nutritional yeast

1 tablespoon fresh lemon juice

¼ teaspoon kosher salt

¼ cup water

1 cup vegetable stock

1 clove garlic, peeled

Special Equipment: Blender

Cashews have a beautiful buttery taste and develop a creamy texture when blended. This "cheesy" cashew cream gets its cheese flavor from nutritional yeast. Don't worry, it doesn't taste like traditional yeast. Its nutty, cheesy flavor makes it a good choice for cheese-flavored substitutes. This recipe is great for tossing with any pasta, including baked favorites like macaroni and cheese.

Place all the ingredients into the blender. Secure the lid and pulse until smooth and creamy.

Storage Instructions Transfer to an airtight container and store in the refrigerator for up to 4 days.

Pea Pesto Garnished with Microgreens

YIELDS 1½ CUPS

PREP TIME: 10 MIN

FLAVOR NOTES:
NUTTY, SAVORY

VEGAN, 30 MIN OR LESS

1 cup packed fresh basil leaves

1 cup cooked green peas

2 cloves garlic, peeled

¼ cup almonds

1 teaspoon fresh lemon juice

¼ teaspoon kosher salt

½ cup extra-virgin olive oil

Microgreens, for garnish

Special Equipment: Food
Processor or Pestle and Mortar

Pesto combinations are only limited by your imagination. This pesto combines sweet cooked green peas with basil and almonds. It's bright, beautiful, and begs to be paired with any pasta. It's very versatile and would also make a great spread for crostini. If you have the time, toast the almonds beforehand for a punch of extra toasty flavor. Garnish the dish with a sprinkling of microgreens.

1   Place the basil, peas, and garlic into a food processor. Pulse to combine. Add the almonds, lemon juice, and salt and pulse to combine.

2   While pulsing, carefully stream the olive oil into the food processor until the mixture fully comes together. Garnish with the microgreens.

Storage Tip When storing pesto in the refrigerator, top off the jar with a little olive oil before sealing.

Storage Instructions Transfer to an airtight container and store in the refrigerator for up to 4 days.

Cauliflower-Walnut "Meat" Sauce

SERVES 6

PREP TIME: 15 MIN
COOK TIME: 30 MIN

FLAVOR NOTES:
SAVORY, RICH

VEGAN

1 medium head cauliflower, cut
  into florets (about 3 cups)

¾ cup walnuts

3 tablespoons extra-virgin olive oil

2 cloves garlic, minced

¼ onion, minced

½ teaspoon kosher salt

¼ teaspoon freshly ground
  black pepper

14½ ounces Italian-style tomatoes

1 (8-ounce) can tomato sauce

Special Equipment: Food Processor

This is a hearty, incredibly "meaty" dish without the meat. Cauliflower is extremely budget-friendly and very versatile. Once the cauliflower head is trimmed and broken into flo-rets, it's placed into the food processor and pulsed until it reaches a "rice" consistency. Then the cauliflower and nuts are mixed with tomatoes and simmered until they form a thick, stewy sauce. This sauce is perfect for chunky short pasta, but dainty pasta would not hold up well.

1 Place the cauliflower into the food processor and pulse until it reaches a "rice" consistency. Set aside. Place the walnuts in the food processor and pulse until they're coarsely chopped.

2 Heat the olive oil in a 5-quart Dutch oven over medium heat. Sauté the garlic and onion until softened, stirring frequently and being careful not to let them burn. Add the cauliflower and walnuts and stir to combine. Cook until the cauliflower has softened.

3 Season with salt and pepper. Add the tomatoes and tomato sauce. Stir to combine.

4 Reduce the heat and cook until warmed through, stirring as necessary.

Time-Saving Tip You can use prepackaged fresh riced cauliflower, which is now available in many grocery stores.

Storage Instructions Transfer to an airtight container and store in the refrigerator for up to 4 days.

Eggplant, Roasted Red Pepper, and Tomato Sauce

SERVES 6

PREP TIME: 10 MIN
COOK TIME: 1 HR 15 MIN

FLAVOR NOTES:
SAVORY, RICH

VEGAN, NUT FREE

1 eggplant, cut in half vertically

2 tablespoons extra-virgin olive oil

¼ onion, minced

2 cloves garlic, minced

1 (12-ounce) jar roasted red bell peppers, drained and chopped

1 teaspoon kosher salt

½ teaspoon freshly ground black pepper

1 cup vegetable stock

14½ ounces diced tomatoes

¼ teaspoon red pepper flakes

Special Equipment: Immersion Blender (optional)

I feel like eggplants are often overlooked at the supermarket. Maybe if we called them aubergines as the British do, they would fare better. This dish is a take on ratatouille: Roasted eggplant and tomatoes are simmered in vegetable stock until the flavors blend. The eggplant can absolutely be roasted ahead of time for convenience, and, if you like your sauce smooth, a quick spin with the immersion blender makes it as smooth as can be.

1 Preheat the oven to 400°F.

2 Line a rimmed baking sheet with a silicone baking mat or parchment paper. Place the eggplant halves on the baking sheet, cut-side down, and pierce the skin with a fork in several places. Bake for 45 minutes, or until tender. When cool enough to handle, remove and discard the skins.

3 Heat the olive oil in a 5-quart Dutch oven over medium heat. Add the onion and garlic and cook until softened, stirring as necessary and being careful not to burn the garlic.

4 Add the roasted red bell peppers and eggplant and season with salt and pepper. Add the stock, tomatoes, and red pepper flakes and stir to combine.

5 If you prefer a smoother sauce, use an immersion blender and blend until smooth.

Option Tip If the sauce is too thick, add additional vegetable stock a little at a time until it reaches your desired consistency.

Storage Instructions Transfer to an airtight container and store in the refrigerator for up to 4 days.

Chickpeas in Spicy Smoked Tomato Sauce

SERVES 4

PREP TIME: 5 MIN
COOK TIME: 30 MIN

FLAVOR NOTE:
SAVORY

VEGAN, ONE POT, NUT FREE

2 tablespoons extra-virgin olive oil
2 cloves garlic, minced
½ onion, minced
1 (15-ounce) can chickpeas, drained
1 (8-ounce) can tomato sauce
½ cup vegetable stock
¼ teaspoon smoked paprika

Smoked paprika gives this dish so much depth. Smoked paprika is the cousin of sweet paprika and is made from pimiento peppers that are dried, smoked, and then ground into a bright red powder. The chickpeas bring a nutty flavor and add texture to this dish that is a nice contrast to the smooth sauce.

1 Heat the olive oil in a heavy-bottomed saucepan over medium heat. Add the garlic and onion and sauté until softened, stirring as necessary.

2 Add the chickpeas, tomato sauce, stock, and paprika. Stir to combine. Reduce the heat to low and simmer until the chickpeas have softened, stirring as necessary.

Storage Instructions Transfer to an airtight container and store in the refrigerator for up to 4 days.

Creamy Tofu Sauce

YIELDS 1½ CUPS

PREP TIME: 5 MIN

FLAVOR NOTES:
SAVORY, RICH, CREAMY

**VEGAN, 30 MIN OR LESS,
5-INGREDIENT**

7 ounces tofu

½ cup almond milk

1 tablespoon nutritional yeast

1 tablespoon lemon juice

½ teaspoon kosher salt

2 tablespoons garlic paste

Special Equipment: Blender

This is a quick and easy 5-minute recipe for a thick, rich, and creamy tofu sauce. When I say easy, I mean easy; it is made entirely in the blender. I use garlic paste for this recipe, but you can substitute whole peeled garlic—just note that fresh will be stronger than paste, so use only 1 tablespoon if you are substituting.

Place all ingredients into the blender. Secure the blender lid and pulse until smooth.

Substitution Tips You can substitute soy milk for almond milk. You can also use your preferred brand and texture/firmness of tofu.
Storage Instructions Transfer to an airtight container and store in the refrigerator for up to 4 days.

CHAPTER 8

BASE DISHES

NOW THAT YOU HAVE A LARGE VARIETY OF pasta sauce recipes at your fingertips and have earmarked your favorites or placed sticky notes throughout the book (because who doesn't love sticky notes?), let's chat about all things pasta and especially pairing pasta with sauces.

There are store-bought pastas and homemade pastas. Pasta comes in different textures, flavors, and cooking times. Store-bought pasta comes in dried and fresh forms, in a variety of shapes, and is readily available. These pastas are obviously very convenient to use.

Homemade pasta is made at home, meaning you can control the ingredients that go into it. Homemade pasta cooks in a fraction of the time that store-bought pasta does. You can find several recipes for homemade pasta on my website (www.BellAlimento.com) if you're interested in exploring making your own noodles from scratch.

Before we can pair our pasta with a sauce, we need to know how to cook it properly. It seems like such a basic, simple step but it is surprisingly one that many people get wrong. Not to worry though, that can easily be avoided.

Here are five tips and tricks for getting perfect pasta:

1   Use a pot large enough to accommodate both the water and pasta. Pasta needs to be submerged in water and needs room to do its thing without being crowded. A stockpot or pasta pot is your best option.

2   Don't skimp on the water. You'll need approximately 4 to 6 quarts of water to cook pasta.

3   Let the water come to a complete boil. That does take a hot minute. I'm not the most patient person either, so to speed that process up, I like to place a lid on the pot. When the water begins boiling, it needs to be salted. *Generously*. Salty is a good thing in this case. The water should taste salty, like the sea. I like to use 2 tablespoons of kosher salt for 4 to 6 quarts of water.

4 Once it's boiling, add the pasta and stir so that the pasta is completely submerged in the water. Cook pasta until it is al dente, or "to the tooth," which means it will have a bite to it. Whatever you do, do not let the pasta overcook; overcooked pasta is gummy. If your pasta turns out gummy—and things do happen sometimes—just start over.

5 Before you drain your cooked pasta, reserve 1 cup of cooked pasta water. This magical starchy water will serve to either help thin your sauce or help the sauce to bind together when the pasta is tossed with it.

Store-bought pasta cooking times vary. The particular shape, how much is in the pot, the stove you're using: All these things come into play. Use the suggested cooking time on the box as a guide. The best way to tell when your pasta is ready is to carefully taste a strand. Throwing it against the wall to see if it sticks will just cause you to have to wipe your surface down—and who wants extra cleanup?

Once the pasta is cooked (and you've reserved your cup of pasta water), drain it. Don't rinse the pasta; we want all of its starchy goodness intact. Now, it's time to pair it with a complementary sauce.

Use the base dish recipes in this chapter as a guide for how to combine different sauces and pastas, realizing that sometimes we're all going to make do with what we have on hand in the pantry. 🍎

Gnocchi with Fried Sage-Olive Oil Sauce with Crispy Prosciutto

SERVES 4

PREP TIME: 5 MIN
COOK TIME: 15 MIN

FLAVOR NOTE:
SAVORY

NUT FREE, ONE POT, KID FRIENDLY, GOOD FOR LEFTOVERS, 30 MIN OR LESS, VEGETARIAN (OPTION)

1 teaspoon kosher salt

1 pound potato gnocchi

Fried Sage–Olive Oil Sauce with Crispy Prosciutto (page 25)

Freshly ground black pepper

Parmesan cheese, grated, for garnish

This light fried sage and olive oil sauce coats the gnocchi beautifully while allowing its flavors to shine. You can easily find packaged potato gnocchi in most grocery stores nationwide. It's the perfect quick lunch or dinner. Pair with a salad for a complete meal.

1 Place a stockpot of water on to boil. Once boiling, add the salt and gnocchi and stir. Cook the gnocchi according to package directions. Once fully cooked, drain the gnocchi.

2 Immediately toss the gnocchi with the prepared sauce until coated. Sprinkle prosciutto and sage leaves on top.

3 Season with a grinding of fresh cracked black pepper and sprinkle with desired amount of Parmesan cheese.

Substitution Tip You can substitute bacon for prosciutto. Easily converts to a vegetarian option by omitting the prosciutto.

Storage Instructions Transfer any leftovers to an airtight container and store in the refrigerator for up to 4 days.

Ricotta-Stuffed Shells with Pressure Cooker Bolognese

SERVES 4

PREP TIME: 15 MIN
COOK TIME: 30 MIN

FLAVOR NOTES:
SAVORY, RICH

NUT FREE, KID FRIENDLY, GOOD FOR LEFTOVERS

Nonstick cooking spray, for greasing the pan

1 pound jumbo shell pasta

2 tablespoons kosher salt

1 cup tomato sauce, divided

1½ cups ricotta cheese

1½ cups Pressure Cooker Bolognese (page 73)

1 cup shredded mozzarella cheese

½ cup grated Parmesan

¼ teaspoon freshly ground black pepper

Special Equipment: Electric Pressure Cooker

This is the perfect recipe to make with any leftover Pressure Cooker Bolognese, because it doesn't require the use of the whole sauce recipe. It's a family-friendly meal that everyone enjoys. Pair with a loaf of bread, a side salad, or green vegetables and you're all set. If you're lucky enough to have leftover stuffed shells, they travel well to the office, and they're even better the next day.

1 Preheat the oven to 350°F.

2 Spray a 9-by-13-inch oven-safe casserole dish with nonstick cooking spray. Set aside.

3 Place a stockpot with water on to boil and season generously with salt. Cook the shells until al dente. Drain.

4 Pour half of the tomato sauce into the bottom of the casserole dish so that it is coated.

5 In a medium bowl, mix the ricotta and prepared Bolognese together. Using a spoon, fill each shell with the sauce-and-cheese mixture. Place shells in a single layer in the casserole dish.

6 Pour remaining tomato sauce over shells, coating as much of the shells as possible. Sprinkle the mozzarella and Parmesan cheeses on top of shells, then season with pepper. Bake for about 30 minutes, or until the cheese is browned and bubbly.

Tool Tip Don't rush when stuffing the shells: You don't want the pasta to tear. I've found the best way to stuff them is with a long iced-tea spoon.
Storage Instructions Transfer to an airtight container and store in the refrigerator for up to 4 days.

Baked Pumpkin Macaroni and Cheese

SERVES 4 TO 6

PREP TIME: 25 MIN
COOK TIME: 20 MIN

FLAVOR NOTES:
SAVORY, RICH

**NUT FREE, KID FRIENDLY,
GOOD FOR LEFTOVERS,
VEGETARIAN**

1 pound macaroni

2 tablespoons kosher salt

4 tablespoons unsalted butter

¼ cup all-purpose flour

1 cup whole milk

⅛ teaspoon ground nutmeg

½ teaspoon kosher salt

¼ teaspoon freshly ground
black pepper

½ cup grated Parmesan cheese

1 cup Pumpkin Sauce with
Crispy Mushrooms (page 87)

2 egg yolks

Who doesn't love macaroni and cheese? This grown-up version uses our savory pumpkin sauce recipe, and it's sensational. If you want a little more texture, consider adding crispy bacon crumbles on the top of the dish once it's finished baking. This dish is hearty enough to be a meal on its own or it can be used as a side dish. Mix the mushrooms into the pasta before baking or sprinkle them on top when it's finished.

1 Place a stockpot of water on to boil. Once boiling, season the water with salt and add the macaroni. Cook the pasta until just shy of al dente. Drain.

2 In a 3.5- or 5-quart French or Dutch oven, melt the butter over medium heat. Add the flour and whisk together until blended. Add the milk and cook, stirring, until the mixture nears a boil. Add the nutmeg and season with salt and pepper. Stir to combine.

3 Reduce the heat to low and continue cooking until the mixture thickens enough to coat the back of a wooden spoon.

4 Remove from the heat. Stir the Parmesan, pumpkin sauce, and egg yolks into the sauce until combined and add the cooked, drained pasta. Toss everything to combine.

5 Spray a 9-by-13-inch oven-safe baking dish with nonstick cooking spray. Pour the mixture into the greased baking dish. Bake for 15 to 20 minutes, or until the top is golden brown.

Substitution Tip If you like texture on your macaroni and cheese, sprinkle ¼ cup panko bread crumbs on the dish before baking.
Storage Instructions Transfer any leftovers to an airtight container and store in the refrigerator for up to 4 days.

Fettuccine with Short Ribs and Bourbon Reduction

SERVES 4

PREP TIME: 5 MIN
COOK TIME: 15 MIN

FLAVOR NOTE:
SAVORY

NUT FREE, GOOD FOR LEFTOVERS, 30 MIN OR LESS

1 pound fettuccine
1 tablespoon kosher salt
Short Ribs with Bourbon
  Reduction (page 78)
Parmesan cheese, grated, for garnish

Braised beef short ribs are incredibly tender and delicious after slow cooking in liquid for a few hours—you won't need a knife to cut through the meat. The bourbon reduction sauce used in this recipe is one of my favorite recipes in this book.

1 Place a stockpot of water on to boil. Once boiling, season the water with salt and add the fettucine. Stir. Cook the pasta according to package directions. Drain.

2 Immediately toss the cooked pasta with the prepared sauce until coated.

3 Place the desired amount of pasta on plate and top each plate with short ribs. Sprinkle with grated Parmesan cheese, if desired.

Ingredient Tip You can serve the short ribs bone-in or you can remove the bone and shred the meat using two forks.
Storage Instructions Transfer any leftovers to an airtight container and store in the refrigerator for up to 4 days.

Orecchiette with Veal Sauce, Grilled Lemons, and Burrata

SERVES 4

PREP TIME: 5 MIN
COOK TIME: 15 MIN

FLAVOR NOTES:
SAVORY, RICH

NUT FREE, ONE POT, KID FRIENDLY, GOOD FOR LEFTOVERS, 30 MIN OR LESS

1 pound orecchiette

1 tablespoon kosher salt

Veal Sauce with Grilled Lemon (page 77)

8 ounces burrata cheese

Burrata cheese is mozzarella that's formed into a balloon shape and filled with curds and cream. It's basically bliss. When you slice into it, the creamy center runs out, and that will mix beautifully with the veal sauce. Don't forget to give the grilled lemon a squeeze over your veal chops. This is a meal in itself and doesn't need much accompaniment besides a nice glass of wine and perhaps a small salad.

1   Place a stockpot of water on to boil. Once boiling, season the water with salt and add the orecchiette. Stir. Cook the pasta according to package directions. Drain.

2   Immediately toss the cooked pasta with the prepared sauce until coated.

3   Place the desired amount of pasta onto each plate. Top each serving with the veal sauce, grilled lemon, and a slice of burrata.

Ingredient Tip Garnish with chopped fresh parsley for color.
Storage Instructions Transfer any leftovers to an airtight container and store in the refrigerator for up to 4 days.

Farfalle with Sun-Dried Tomato Pesto, Walnuts, and Black Pepper

SERVES 4

PREP TIME: 5 MIN
COOK TIME: 15 MIN

FLAVOR NOTES:
SAVORY, RICH

ONE POT, KID FRIENDLY, GOOD FOR LEFTOVERS, 30 MIN OR LESS, VEGETARIAN

1 pound farfalle pasta

1 tablespoon kosher salt

Sun-Dried Tomato Pesto with Walnuts and Black Pepper (page 65)

Parmesan cheese, grated, for garnish

If you want a fast meal or pasta salad, it doesn't get any easier than this, especially if you have the pesto premade. Farfalle (butterflies or bow ties, depending on where you're from) is a great pasta choice to accompany pesto. Once the pasta is cooked, simply toss with the pesto. Garnish with additional chopped nuts and a sprinkling of cheese. Want to beef it up? Add a cooked, sliced chicken breast to the top of the pasta, along with a side of steamed asparagus or your favorite vegetable, for a complete meal.

1   Place a stockpot of water on to boil. Once boiling, season the water with salt and add the farfalle. Stir. Cook the pasta according to package directions. Drain.

2   Immediately toss cooked pasta with the prepared pesto until coated.

3   Place the desired amount of pasta onto each plate. Top with grated Parmesan for garnish.

Ingredient Tips This pasta salad can be served either hot or cold. Swap out the farfalle for fusilli. Pesto sticks to the ridges of their corkscrew shape beautifully.

Storage Instructions Transfer any leftovers to an airtight container and store in the refrigerator for up to 4 days.

Spinach and "Cheesy" Cashew Sauce Lasagna

SERVES 6

PREP TIME: 15 MIN
COOK TIME: 45 MIN

FLAVOR NOTES:
SAVORY, RICH

**VEGETARIAN, KID FRIENDLY,
GOOD FOR LEFTOVERS**

Nonstick cooking spray,
  for greasing the pan

4 tablespoons unsalted butter

⅓ onion, minced

2 cloves garlic, minced

20 ounces frozen spinach, thawed,
  drained and squeezed of all liquid

½ teaspoon kosher salt, divided

½ teaspoon freshly ground
  black pepper, divided

15 ounces whole ricotta

1 egg

"Cheesy" Cashew Cream
  Sauce (page 90)

1 (9-ounce) box oven-ready
  lasagna noodles

2 cups shredded mozzarella

Lasagna is always a crowd favorite. This is a vegetarian version that makes use of our "Cheesy" Cashew Cream Sauce, which we use instead of a traditional béchamel sauce. I've taken a shortcut by using oven-ready lasagna noodles. That means no boiling pasta. The trick is to make sure the noodles are covered in sauce so they cook all the way through.

1 Preheat the oven to 400°F.

2 Spray a 9-by-13-inch oven-safe baking dish with nonstick cooking spray. Set aside.

3 Heat the butter in a large skillet over medium heat. Add the onion and garlic and cook until softened. Add the spinach and season with salt and pepper. Cook until the spinach is warmed through.

4 In a medium bowl, mix the ricotta and egg and season with salt and pepper. Using a slotted spoon, transfer the spinach mixture into the ricotta mixture. Stir well to combine.

5 To assemble: Place just enough cashew cream sauce onto the bottom of the prepared dish to coat it. Top with 3 lasagna noodles. Spread ⅓ of the spinach mixture on top of the noodles, then top with ⅓ of the cashew–cream sauce mixture and ⅓ of the mozzarella. Continue the process for 2 additional layers.

6 Cover the dish with foil. Bake for 30 minutes, then carefully remove the foil and continue baking for an additional 15 minutes, or until the cheese is browned and bubbly.

Helpful Tip Be sure you squeeze all the excess water from the spinach. You don't want any extra liquid making your lasagna soggy.
Storage Instructions Transfer any leftovers to an airtight container and store in the refrigerator for up to 4 days.

Grilled Spring Onion Pesto with Penne Pasta and Chicken

SERVES 4

PREP TIME: 5 MIN
COOK TIME: 15 MIN

FLAVOR NOTES:
SAVORY, RICH

**GOOD FOR LEFTOVERS,
DAIRY FREE, 30 MIN OR LESS**

1 pound penne

2 tablespoons kosher salt

Grilled Spring Onion Pesto (page 66)

4 chicken breasts

1 teaspoon kosher salt

¼ teaspoon freshly ground black pepper

Parmesan cheese, grated, for garnish

This is another quick and easy weeknight dinner. You will already be grilling the spring onion, so it's the perfect time to grill up a few chicken breasts to go with the meal. Grilled salmon would be a great option as well. While the pasta is cooking, grill the meat so that everything is ready at the same time.

1   Place a stockpot of water on to boil. Once boiling, season the water with salt and add the penne. Stir. Cook the pasta according to package directions. Drain.

2   Immediately toss the cooked pasta with the prepared pesto until coated (see Helpful Tips below).

3   Season the chicken with salt and pepper on both sides. Heat a grill pan over medium-high heat. Add chicken and cook 5 or 6 minutes on the first side. Using tongs, flip and continue cooking until juices run clear. Cooking time will depend on the thickness of the chicken breast. Remove from the heat and allow the chicken to rest prior to slicing.

4   Place the desired amount of pasta onto each plate. Top each serving with grilled chicken and grated Parmesan.

Helpful Tips   You can substitute any pesto recipe in the book for the Grilled Spring Onion Pesto.
If the pasta seems a little dry after tossing with the pesto, mix in a little reserved pasta water.
Storage Instructions   Transfer any leftovers to an airtight container and store in the refrigerator for up to 4 days.

Bucatini with Tomato-Goat Cheese Blender Sauce

SERVES 4

PREP TIME: 5 MIN
COOK TIME: 15 MIN

FLAVOR NOTES:
SAVORY, RICH

**GOOD FOR LEFTOVERS,
5 INGREDIENTS OR LESS, 30 MIN
OR LESS, NUT FREE (OPTION)**

1 pound bucatini

2 tablespoons kosher salt

Blender Creamy Tomato Sauce
  with Goat Cheese (page 32)

1 tablespoon crushed walnuts

Parmesan cheese, grated, for garnish

Bucatini is a long, hollow pasta; think of it as the pasta straw. It's a clunky twirler, but it's definitely fun to eat. Since the sauce is made in a blender, this meal comes together in about 15 minutes. If you want to add a protein to the plate, consider shrimp!

1 Place a stockpot of water on to boil. Once boiling, season the water with salt and add the bucatini. Stir. Cook the pasta according to package directions. Drain.

2 Immediately toss the cooked pasta with the prepared sauce until coated (see Helpful Tips below).

3 Place the desired amount of pasta onto each plate. Top each serving with crushed walnuts and grated Parmesan cheese.

Helpful Tips If the pasta seems a bit dry after tossing with the sauce, mix in a little reserved pasta water. If you prefer this to be nut-free, simply omit the walnuts and use thinly sliced basil instead.

Storage Instructions Transfer any leftovers to an airtight container and store in the refrigerator for up to 4 days.

Spaghetti with Squash Carbonara

SERVES 4

PREP TIME: 5 MIN
COOK TIME: 15 MIN

FLAVOR NOTES:
SAVORY, RICH

GOOD FOR LEFTOVERS,
5 INGREDIENTS OR LESS,
30 MIN OR LESS

1 pound spaghetti

2 tablespoons kosher salt

Squash Carbonara with
  Pancetta (page 72)

Parmesan cheese, grated, for garnish

Spaghetti alla carbonara is rich and indulgent. Adding a seasonal squash to the mix is a modern twist on this classic. Be mindful of the cooking instructions on the sauce, as timing is crucial for this recipe. Add some crusty Italian bread and wine, and you're all set.

1 Place a stockpot of water on to boil. Once boiling, season the water with salt and add the spaghetti. Stir. Cook the pasta according to package directions. Drain.

2 Toss the cooked pasta with the prepared sauce immediately (see sauce recipe instructions for specific procedure).

3 Garnish with grated Parmesan. Serve immediately.

Time-Saving Tip If you roast the squash for the sauce recipe ahead of time, this comes together very quickly.

Storage Instructions Transfer any leftovers to an airtight container and store in the refrigerator for up to 4 days.

MEASUREMENT CONVERSIONS

VOLUME EQUIVALENTS (LIQUID)

U.S. STANDARD	U.S. STANDARD (OUNCES)	METRIC (APPROXIMATE)
2 tablespoons	1 fl. oz.	30 mL
¼ cup	2 fl. oz.	60 mL
½ cup	4 fl. oz.	120 mL
1 cup	8 fl. oz.	240 mL
1½ cups	12 fl. oz.	355 mL
2 cups or 1 pint	16 fl. oz.	475 mL
4 cups or 1 quart	32 fl. oz.	1 L
1 gallon	128 fl. oz.	4 L

OVEN TEMPERATURES

FAHRENHEIT (F)	CELSIUS (C) (APPROXIMATE)
250°F	120°C
300°F	150°C
325°F	165°C
350°F	180°C
375°F	190°C
400°F	200°C
425°F	220°C
450°F	230°C

VOLUME EQUIVALENTS (DRY)

U.S. STANDARD	METRIC (APPROXIMATE)
⅛ teaspoon	0.5 mL
¼ teaspoon	1 mL
½ teaspoon	2 mL
¾ teaspoon	4 mL
1 teaspoon	5 mL
1 tablespoon	15 mL
¼ cup	59 mL
⅓ cup	79 mL
½ cup	118 mL
⅔ cup	156 mL
¾ cup	177 mL
1 cup	235 mL
2 cups or 1 pint	475 mL
3 cups	700 mL
4 cups or 1 quart	1 L

WEIGHT EQUIVALENTS

U.S. STANDARD	METRIC (APPROXIMATE)
½ ounce	15 g
1 ounce	30 g
2 ounces	60 g
4 ounces	115 g
8 ounces	225 g
12 ounces	340 g
16 ounces or 1 pound	455 g

RESOURCES

Websites:

bellalimento.com

LaCucinaItaliana.com

LidiasItaly.com

Cookbooks:

The Silver Spoon

Essentials of Classic Italian Cooking by Marcella Hazan

INDEX

INDEX

INDEX

INDEX

INDEX

INDEX

INDEX

ACKNOWLEDGMENTS

Many thanks to . . .

My mother, to whom this book is dedicated. Without her propping me up on a chair in the kitchen when I was barely tall enough to reach the counter, teaching me all about real food and home cooking, I don't believe I would have the love and passion for cooking that I do now. She was my greatest teacher and cheerleader. There aren't enough words or ways to thank her for everything she did to love, encourage, and support me.

To my incredible family, this book wouldn't be possible without you. Thank you for loving me enough to taste everything I ever put in front of you, for washing endless amounts of dishes, and for always waiting to eat until I photographed the food, albeit while rolling your eyes. Y'all are simply the best, and I can always count on you to be the most brutally honest reviewers in the history of food critics. I love y'all to the moon and back.

To my best friend, who is the most aca-awesome nerd, cheesecake crusher, coconspirator, and amazing cocktail maker a girl could ever hope to know.

To my friends, thank you for always showing up for me. For letting me talk your ears off no matter what time it was. For sending ridiculous GIFs that make me lol at the most awkward times. You are my tribe.

To the readers of *Bell'Alimento*, I appreciate each and every one of you. Thank you for inspiring me and especially for your ongoing support over the past 10 years.

I'm not crying. You're crying.

ABOUT THE AUTHOR

Paula Jones is a professional recipe developer, food writer, food photographer, and founder of the popular website *BellAlimento.com*, a food blog celebrating simple, seasonal, family-friendly recipes for the past 10 years.

Paula has written and developed recipes for her website, as well as for many companies and brands. Her clients include large national brands, public relations firms, and small family-run businesses.

Paula's work has appeared in numerous online publications and in various print media, such as *Southern Living* magazine, and has been nominated for the *Saveur* Best Food Blog Award. Paula lives in Raleigh, North Carolina.

CPSIA information can be obtained
at www.ICGtesting.com
Printed in the USA
BVHW022346051119
563009BV00002B/13/P

9 781641 529907